Unlock Your Superpowers

Embrace Your Leadership Journey and Unleash Your True Potential

By

Bonnie M. Bruce

Table of Contents

Explore the profound impact of trust on our personal and professional lives. Together, we'll discover how trust forms the bedrock of meaningful relationships, fuels collaboration, and unlocks the doors to growth and success.

Assess the transformative force of respect. Discover how respect serves as the catalyst for empathy, understanding, and cooperation in both personal and professional lives. Together, we'll unveil the remarkable ways in which respect shapes our interactions, fosters inclusivity, and paves the way for a world where dignity and collaboration reign supreme.

Analyze the profound significance of integrity in shaping character and building trust. Dive into the essence of integrity as the cornerstone of authenticity and ethical behavior in our personal and professional lives. Together, we'll uncover how integrity serves as the moral compass guiding our decisions and actions, ultimately leading us towards a path of honor, reliability, and lasting success.

Delve into the transformative force of empathy. Explore how empathy is the key to understanding, connecting with, and positively impacting the lives of others. Together, we'll discover how cultivating empathy allows us to bridge gaps, strengthen relationships, and foster a world where compassion and understanding prevail.

Unit 5 - The Power of Humility

Contemplate how humility serves as the foundation for continuous learning, collaboration, and personal development. Together, we'll uncover how embracing humility not only nurtures self-awareness but also opens doors to meaningful connections and lasting success, reminding us that greatness often begins with a humble heart.

Unit 6 - The Power of Courage

Discover how courage empowers individuals to confront challenges, overcome obstacles, and chart new horizons. Together, we'll reveal how embracing courage is the catalyst for personal and professional growth, enabling us to rise above adversity and make a lasting impact on the world.

Unit 7 - The Power of Resilience

Explore how resilience allows individuals to bounce back from setbacks, adapt to change, and thrive in the face of adversity. Together, we'll uncover how cultivating resilience equips us with the ability to weather life's storms, emerge stronger, and transform challenges into opportunities for growth and triumph.

Unit 8 – The Power of Empowerment

Consider how empowerment unlocks human potential, fosters growth, and ignites positive change in individuals and communities. Together, we'll uncover how the act of empowering others and ourselves is not only a path to personal fulfillment but also a catalyst for creating a brighter, more inclusive future.

Unit 9 - The Power of Communication

Examine how effective communication is the cornerstone of connection, collaboration, and understanding in our personal and professional lives. Together, we'll uncover how mastering the art of communication can bridge gaps, resolve conflicts, and pave the way for stronger relationships and successful endeavors.

Unit 10 - The Power of Accountability

Learn how accountability is the linchpin of personal and professional growth, fostering responsibility and integrity. Together, we'll reveal how embracing accountability empowers us to own our actions, achieve our goals, and build a culture of trust and excellence.

Unit 11 - The Power of Adaptability

Evaluate how adaptability equips us to thrive in an ever-changing world, embrace new challenges, and seize opportunities for growth. Together, we'll uncover how cultivating adaptability is not just a skill but a mindset that empowers us to navigate uncertainty with confidence and resilience.

Unit 12 - The Power of Collaboration

Explore how collaboration transcends boundaries, ignites innovation, and fosters synergy among individuals and teams. Through compelling stories and actionable insights, we'll uncover how embracing collaboration is the key to unlocking collective potential, achieving shared goals, and creating a future built on unity and shared success.

Unit 13 - The Power of Inclusion

Investigate how inclusion transcends differences, celebrates diversity, and fosters a sense of belonging in our communities and organizations. Together, we'll uncover how practicing inclusion not only enriches lives but also empowers us to create equitable, vibrant, and compassionate environments where every voice is valued and heard.

Unit 14 - The Power of Mentorship

In this inspiring unit, we delve into the transformative influence of mentorship. Explore how mentorship bridges knowledge gaps, nurtures growth, and empowers individuals to reach their full potential. Together, we'll reveal how the guidance and wisdom of mentors can light the path to success, providing invaluable support and inspiration on the journey toward personal and professional fulfillment.

Conclusion

About the Author

Dedication

To my loving husband,

Thank you for your unwavering support and encouragement during the writing of this book. Your dedication and belief in me have inspired and driven my passion for leadership and personal development. Your commitment to being a positive role model, not only for our family but also for those around us, has been a guiding light in my journey toward creating meaningful change.

This book is dedicated to you, my partner in life and love. Thank you for being my rock, confidant, and greatest supporter.

Acknowledgments

A heartfelt thanks to my late mother, Nancy Marchitto, for her inspiration and guidance throughout her life, which will continue throughout mine.

I would like to express my deep appreciation to my beloved daughters, Shelley and Melissa, my son-in-law, Brent, and my dear grandchildren, Emma and Cody, as well as my sons, Brian and Nathan. Their unwavering love, support, and presence in my life bring immense joy and serve as a constant reminder of the significance of family. I am truly grateful to have them in my life.

Introduction

The concept behind this workbook unfolds in four dimensions. Readers have the option to convene and establish a Mastermind Group, be guided by a facilitator, engage in discussions with friends to glean insights from one another or use it as a personal tool to enhance your leadership skills. Workbooks encompass diverse objectives, contingent on the reader's aspirations and the goals they aim to accomplish by engaging with its content.

As we begin this journey into the world of leadership, we often hear about superpowers that come from fictional characters, such as flying or teleporting. But what about the real-life superpowers that leaders possess? This thought inspired me to write this workbook, which focuses on the essential superpowers of leadership, which are the qualities and characteristics that make great leaders stand out from the rest.

Through real-life stories and practical thought-provoking questions, we will delve into the key traits that make a powerful leader, from empathy and communication to resilience and adaptability.

Whether you hold an executive role, are a new manager, or aspire to become a leader, its purpose is to help you cultivate the skills and mindset needed for personal growth and success. By understanding and harnessing the superpowers of leadership, you can inspire and empower your team to achieve remarkable outcomes. Join me on this journey as we explore the realm of leadership and unleash our true potential together.

Before we commence, I'd like to provide you with tools to optimize your journey towards effective leadership.

The Power of the Four P's

"Fortune favors the prepared mind." - Louis Pasteur

Let's explore the four P's, a set of principles that can be applied not only in training classes but also in various aspects of life, such as job interviews, presentations, webinars, and more. These principles are valuable tools that can enhance your effectiveness and success in different situations. Let's delve into each of them and uncover their significance in empowering you to achieve your goals.

Be Prepared: As a leader, the most important step toward growth is being prepared. This involves reading assignments, articles, listening to podcasts and TED Talks related to the subject you aim to master. Being prepared is the foundation for your learning and development.

Be Present: With the abundance of technology, it's easy to lose focus and check emails, texts, or chat during meetings or training sessions. Being present and in the moment makes all the difference between learning and retaining information or getting distracted. Your mindset is key, and during this time, nothing else should matter.

Participate: To grow on your learning journey, it's essential to participate and share your voice. Everyone has a unique story to tell and experiences to share. Participating in discussions and activities enables you to learn more about yourself and others.

Practice: Practicing what you have learned is crucial to retaining new knowledge. If you have prepared, are present, and participate, you will not want to waste what you have learned. Apply your newfound knowledge in real-life situations to cement your understanding.

Applying the Four P's

"By failing to prepare, you are preparing to fail."
- Benjamin Franklin

1. How can being prepared before a learning session enhance your overall understanding and growth as a leader?

_____

_____

_____

2. Reflect on a time when you were fully present during a meeting or training. How did it impact your learning experience?

_____

_____

_____

3. In what ways does technology affect your ability to stay present and engaged during learning sessions?

_____

_____

_____

4. Why is having the right mindset important for maximizing your learning during meetings or training?

_____

_____

_____

5. How does active participation contribute to your personal growth and learning as a leader?

_____

_____

_____

6. Think about a recent discussion or activity you participated in. How did it broaden your perspective and add to your understanding?

_____

_____

_____

7. Can you recall a situation where you didn't actively participate? How did it affect your learning experience?

_____

_____

_____

8. How do you plan to practice and apply what you've learned in real-life scenarios?

_____

_____

_____

9. Share an example of how applying new knowledge in a practical situation has improved your leadership skills.

_____

_____

_____

10. What strategies can you employ to ensure that you remain present and engaged during learning sessions, even when distractions arise?

_____

_____

_____

The Power of SMART Goals

"A goal properly set is halfway reached." - Zig Ziglar

Specific: SMART goals should be clear and specific, providing a clear description of what needs to be achieved. This helps in focusing efforts and avoiding ambiguity.

Measurable: Goals should be measurable, meaning that there should be a way to track progress and determine if the goal has been achieved. Measurable goals provide a sense of direction and enable the evaluation of success.

Achievable: Goals should be realistic and attainable within the given resources, capabilities, and constraints. They should challenge individuals to grow and stretch their abilities but not be so overwhelming that the person becomes demotivated.

Relevant: Goals should be aligned with the overall objectives and priorities of the individual or organization. They should contribute to the larger picture and have a meaningful impact.

Time-bound: Goals should have a specific timeline or deadline for completion. This creates a sense of urgency and helps in prioritizing tasks and managing time effectively.

Applying SMART Goals

"Setting goals is the first step in turning the invisible into the visible." - Tony Robbins

1. Why is setting goals important for achieving success?

_____

_____

_____

2. How can the SMART criteria help you set achievable goals?

_____

_____

_____

3. What are some examples of specific, measurable, and time-bound goals?

_____

_____

_____

4. What is the importance of setting realistic goals?

_____

_____

_____

5. How can breaking down a goal into smaller tasks help you achieve it?

_____

_____

_____

6. What are some strategies for tracking progress towards your goals?

_____

_____

_____

7. How can sharing your goals with others help you stay accountable?

_____

_____

_____

8. How can you adjust your goals as circumstances change?

_____

_____

_____

9. What is the benefit of celebrating your achievements as you reach your goals?

_____

_____

_____

10. Outline your professional and personal aspirations for the upcoming five years.

_____

_____

_____

Remember that setting SMART goals is not a solitary act but a harmonious symphony when combined with preparedness, presence, participation, and practice. It is in this orchestration that we find our true potential as leaders.

Let us embark on our leadership journeys armed with SMART goals, preparedness for the road ahead, an unwavering presence in each moment, active participation in our teams, and a dedication to practice what we've learned. Together, we shall not only unlock our superpowers of leadership but also inspire those around us to do the same.

Unit 1
The Power of Trust

"The glue that holds all relationships together - including the relationship between the leader and the led - is trust, and trust is based on integrity." - Brian Tracy

Trust is a fundamental element of effective leadership. It is the glue that binds teams and organizations together and enables them to achieve shared goals. Leaders trusted by their team members can build strong relationships, inspire confidence, and create a culture of collaboration and innovation. Trust is an exchange that flows both ways. Leaders should extend trust to their team members just as they desire to be trusted themselves. When mutual trust exists, it creates an atmosphere of empowerment and accountability, allowing individuals to take the initiative and offer their most valuable insights and contributions.

In this Unit, we will explore the importance of trust in leadership and how it can be developed and maintained over time. We will examine the key factors that contribute to trust, such as honesty, transparency, and reliability, and explore the consequences of a lack of trust, including low morale, decreased productivity, and high turnover.

Through stories and examples, we will learn from leaders who have successfully built and maintained trust within their teams and organizations. By the end of this Unit, you will have a deeper understanding of the critical role that trust plays in effective leadership and the practical steps you can take to build and maintain trust with those you lead.

Attributes of Trust

"The best leaders are those who build trust with their followers by being transparent, honest, and authentic in their actions and words." - Unknown

Honesty: Being honest is important in building trust because it creates a sense of integrity and credibility. When leaders are honest with their employees, they show that they value transparency and that they can be trusted to tell the truth. Transparency in leadership does not mean compromising confidentiality. Rather, it entails cultivating a culture of openness and honesty with employees. By demonstrating the importance of transparency, leaders show their commitment to building trust and being trustworthy in delivering the truth. This helps to establish an open and respectful communication culture within the organization. Additionally, being honest about failures and mistakes can help leaders work collaboratively with their employees to find solutions and improve processes. Overall, honesty is a key factor in building and maintaining a trusting relationship between leaders and their employees.

Empathy: Leaders who show empathy and understanding towards their employees are more likely to be trusted. Demonstrating empathy is crucial for leaders as it helps establish trust and promote positive connections with employees. By showing empathy, leaders convey their genuine concern toward employees and their willingness to understand their viewpoints and experiences. This, in turn, results in greater employee satisfaction and loyalty, improved communication, and enhanced collaboration within the team. Displaying empathy contributes to fostering a positive work environment where employees feel appreciated and supported. Showing empathy plays a vital role in promoting effective leadership and can significantly influence employee morale and performance.

Leading by example: Leaders who set a positive example and demonstrate the behaviors they expect from their employees are more likely to be trusted. This is because when employees see their leaders modeling a commitment to excellence and integrity, they are motivated to do the same. This can lead to increased productivity, higher job satisfaction, and a greater sense of pride in their work. By demonstrating a strong work ethic, treating others with respect, and upholding the values and principles of the organization, leaders can inspire their employees to follow suit and create a positive work culture.

Clear communication: Clear communication can also help to promote a positive and inclusive workplace culture. When leaders communicate clearly and openly, it can help to build a sense of transparency and trust within the organization. This can create an environment where employees feel comfortable sharing their opinions and ideas, and there is a greater sense of collaboration and teamwork. In addition, clear communication can help promote diversity and inclusion by ensuring that all employees have access to the same information and can contribute to the organization's goals and objectives. Overall, clear communication is a critical component of effective leadership and can significantly impact organizational success, employee morale, and trust.

Accountability: Leaders who hold themselves accountable and take responsibility for their actions are more likely to gain the trust of their employees. It demonstrates their integrity and commitment to the organization's values, leading to increased respect and admiration from employees. Accountability also fosters transparency and trust within the organization, creating a safe environment for employees to speak up about their mistakes and concerns. Conversely, leaders who avoid accountability can damage trust, leading to low morale and decreased productivity. Leaders who take accountability are crucial for fostering a positive work environment.

Respect: Leaders who demonstrate respect towards all employees, regardless of their position or background, are more likely to build positive relationships and gain the trust of their team. When leaders show respect, they value the perspectives and contributions of their employees, creating a work environment where everyone feels valued and heard. This can result in increased motivation, job satisfaction, and improved morale among employees. Showing respect can also promote a culture of collaboration and teamwork, leading to better communication and problem-solving.

By treating others with dignity and kindness, leaders can set an example for their employees to follow, creating a positive and productive work environment.

Demonstrating Trust

"A leader's job is to inspire and empower others, and that can only happen if there is trust between the leader and their team."
- Simon Sinek

1. Describe a time when you had to trust someone else to complete an important task or project. How did you feel about putting your trust in him or her?

_____

_____

_____

2. Have you ever been in a situation where you felt that someone had betrayed your trust? How did you respond to that situation, and what did you learn from it?

_____

_____

_____

3. Can you think of a time when you had to rebuild trust with someone after a breach of trust had occurred? What steps did you take to repair the relationship?

_____

_____

_____

4. How do you determine if someone is trustworthy? What qualities do you look for when deciding whether to trust a person?

_____

_____

_____

5. Have you ever had to trust your instincts when deciding about someone's trustworthiness? Can you describe the situation and how you arrived at your decision?

_____

_____

_____

6. Can you think of a time when you had to earn someone else's trust? How did you go about building that trust, and what strategies did you use?

_____

_____

_____

7. How important is trust to you in your personal and professional relationships? What steps do you take to build and maintain trust with others?

_____

_____

_____

A Captain's Trust

"Trust is a leader's currency. With it, he or she is solvent; without it, he or she is bankrupt." - Jack Welch

In the heart of the North Atlantic, aboard the USS Horizon, Captain Amelia Winters led her crew through a relentless storm. The waves crashed against the ship, and the howling wind made communication nearly impossible. But amidst the chaos, a story of trust was about to unfold that would forever be etched in the memories of those on board.

Captain Winters was known for her steadfast leadership and unwavering trust in her crew. Her belief in their abilities had instilled a sense of confidence that resonated throughout the ship. As the storm raged on, the crew faced one of the most challenging situations they had ever encountered.

Amid the chaos, the ship's communication systems faltered, leaving them cut off from the outside world. The navigational instruments were haywire, and the crew found themselves relying on their instincts and skills to navigate the treacherous waters.

As the storm intensified, Captain Winters called a meeting with her officers. In the dimly lit conference room, the crew gathered, their faces etched with worry. Captain Winters stood at the head of the table, her presence calming despite the circumstances.

"We're facing a situation none of us expected," she began, her voice steady. "Our instruments are down, and communication is limited. But we've trained for scenarios like this. Our training, our teamwork, that's what will guide us through this storm."

The crew exchanged glances, their faith in Captain Winters evident. She continued, "I trust each and every one of you. We're a team, and together, we can overcome any challenge. Remember, the sea might be relentless, but so are we."

For days, the crew battled the storm with a determination fueled by their captain's trust. They worked tirelessly, relying on their instincts, knowledge, and each other. As they faced enormous waves and turbulent winds, their bond grew stronger.

Amidst the turmoil, Chief Engineer Jackson discovered a way to restore limited communication using unconventional methods. With a mix of technical expertise and creativity, he managed to send out a distress signal, informing nearby vessels of their situation.

As the days passed, the storm began to relent. Weary but resolute, the crew continued their efforts, guided by Captain Winters' unyielding trust. Their determination paid off when a distant ship responded to the distress signal, guiding them to calmer waters.

With the storm behind them, Captain Winters gathered her crew on the deck. The sun broke through the clouds, casting a warm glow on their tired faces. She spoke, her voice carrying a mix of relief and pride, "We've been through one of the toughest challenges we could face at sea. And it's not just our skills that got us through; it's the trust we have in each other. Your dedication, your resilience, it's what makes this crew exceptional."

The crew exchanged smiles, their bond stronger than ever. Captain Winters' trust in them had not only helped them overcome a physical storm but had also solidified their unity as a team. From that day forward, the story of Captain Winters' demonstration of trust echoed through the ship's corridors, a testament to the power of belief in the face of adversity.

Unbreakable Trust

"Trust is the glue of life. It is an essential ingredient in effective communication. It's the foundational principle that holds all relationships." - Stephen Covey

Alan Mulally's tenure as CEO of Ford from 2006 to 2014 is a prime example of how a leader can earn the trust of employees and investors through transparent communication, strategic decision-making, and a commitment to teamwork.

When Mulally joined Ford, the company was facing severe financial challenges and a declining market share. One of the first things he did was to implement a weekly meeting known as the "Business Plan Review" or "BPR" meeting. In these meetings, Mulally insisted on open and honest discussions about the company's problems and progress. He encouraged his team to share both good and bad news, creating an atmosphere of transparency.

Mulally's approach to leadership was grounded in teamwork and collaboration. He emphasized that the success of the company was a collective effort and that everyone's input was valuable. This was a significant departure from the traditional top-down approach in the automotive industry. Mulally's willingness to listen and value his team's expertise helped foster a sense of ownership and engagement among employees.

During a critical period when the company was at risk of bankruptcy, Mulally secured a line of credit to provide financial stability. Instead of merely using Ford's assets as collateral, he additionally utilized the company's iconic Blue Oval logo as leverage. This strategic move showcased Mulally's determination to preserve the company's legacy and rebuild trust in its brand.

Mulally's leadership was not just about numbers and financial decisions; it was about fostering a culture of trust and collaboration. He believed that by working together and being honest about challenges, the company could overcome any obstacles.

His efforts paid off. Under Mulally's leadership, Ford not only survived the global financial crisis but also underwent a significant transformation. The company streamlined its operations, focused on producing more fuel-efficient vehicles, and invested in innovation. Ford's financial health improved, and it became a symbol of resilience in the automotive industry.

Alan Mulally's success at Ford was attributed not only to his strategic brilliance but also to his ability to gain the trust of employees and investors. His transparent communication, collaborative approach, and commitment to the company's values and legacy created a culture of trust that propelled Ford's turnaround. His leadership legacy serves as a testament to how building trust can drive remarkable transformation and success.

Applying Trust

"The function of leadership is to produce more leaders, not more followers. Trust is the essence of leadership, and people who trust you will follow you." - Tony Blair

1. Think about a time in your leadership journey when building trust was crucial to achieving a significant goal. Can you describe the situation and the steps you took to establish trust among your team members?

_____

_____

_____

2. In the story of Captain Winters, trust played a pivotal role in the success of his unit. Can you share a leadership experience where trust was a defining factor in overcoming adversity or challenges?

_____

_____

_____

3. Alan Mulally emphasized transparency and open communication to build trust within Ford. Can you provide an example from your leadership where transparent communication helped foster trust and alignment among your team members?

_____

_____

_____

4. Reflect on a time when trust within your team was tested due to a mistake or setback. How did you handle the situation to rebuild trust and maintain team morale?

_____

_____

_____

5. Both stories highlight the importance of consistency in leadership to establish and maintain trust. Can you discuss how you've consistently demonstrated trustworthiness throughout your leadership journey?

_____

_____

_____

Unit 2
The Power of Respect

"If you want to be respected as a leader, be consistent in your behavior and treat everyone with fairness and dignity." - Unknown

Respect is a foundational aspect of effective leadership. When leaders show respect to their team members, they build trust, foster positive relationships, and create a culture of mutual support and collaboration.

In this Unit, we will explore the importance of respect in leadership and how it can be demonstrated in both words and actions. We will examine the benefits of a respectful workplace, the consequences of disrespectful behavior, and strategies for promoting a culture of respect within your team or organization.

Through stories and examples, we will learn from leaders who have demonstrated respect in their leadership and have created environments where everyone feels valued and heard.

By the end of this Unit, you will have a deeper understanding of the critical role that respect plays in leadership and the practical steps you can take to show respect to those you lead.

So, let us explore the power of respect and discover how we can harness its potential to create a more positive and successful workplace.

Attributes of Respect

"People will forget what you said, people will forget what you did, but people will never forget how you made them feel."
- Maya Angelou

Active Listening: Pay attention to what others have to say and show genuine interest in their ideas, thoughts, and opinions.

Empathy: Try to understand and appreciate the feelings and perspectives of others and be supportive of their needs and concerns.

Acknowledge Accomplishments: Recognize and celebrate the accomplishments of your team members and show appreciation for their hard work and dedication.

Create an Inclusive Environment: Foster a culture of inclusion, diversity, and belonging where everyone feels valued, respected, and heard.

Treat Others Equally: Be fair and consistent in your interactions with team members and avoid showing favoritism.

Value Differences: Appreciate and embrace differences in backgrounds, experiences, and perspectives and use them as a source of strength and innovation.

Respect Boundaries: Be mindful of others' boundaries and personal space and avoid making assumptions or judgments based on stereotypes or biases.

Demonstrating Respect

"When people respect you as a person, they admire you. When they respect you as a friend, they love you. When they respect you as a leader, they follow you." - John C. Maxwell

1. Reflect on a time when you felt respected by someone. What did they do or say that made you feel that way?

_____

_____

_____

2. Have you ever experienced disrespect in a professional or personal setting? How did it make you feel, and how did you respond to it?

_____

_____

_____

3. Can you give an example of a situation where you had to demonstrate respect towards someone with whom you had a disagreement or conflict? How did you handle the situation?

_____

_____

_____

4. How do you think showing respect towards others can impact the quality of your relationships, both personally and professionally?

_____

_____

_____

5. In your opinion, what are some key qualities or behaviors that are indicative of a person who values respect?

_____

_____

_____

6. How do you typically respond when someone shows disrespect towards you or someone else? What strategies have you found to be effective in these situations?

_____

_____

_____

7. Can you think of a time when you had to navigate a cultural or linguistic difference to show respect towards someone? How did you handle the situation, and what did you learn from it?

_____

_____

_____

Respect Can Inspire and Unite People

"Respect is the key determinant of high-performance leadership. How much people respect you determines how well they perform." - Brian Tracy

While living in Tampa during Tony Dungy's time as head coach of the Tampa Bay Buccaneers, I witnessed his impact on the community. Dungy was a respected figure and philanthropist and exemplified strong leadership and character.

Dungy had a successful career as an NFL (National Football League) coach and player. He played for the Pittsburgh Steelers, San Francisco 49ers, and the New York Giants as a defensive back after playing quarterback for the Golden Gophers football team at the University of Minnesota. He retired from playing in 1980 and began his coaching career as an assistant coach for his alma mater and then moved on to the NFL.

As head coach of the Buccaneers, Dungy led the team to the playoffs four times in six seasons and was deeply involved in the Tampa Bay community, supporting various charitable organizations and promoting education. Despite being fired in 2001, his legacy continued to inspire respect and admiration.

Dungy was then hired as the head coach of the Indianapolis Colts in 2002, leading the team to even greater success, including a Super Bowl victory in 2007. He retired from coaching in 2009 with a career record of 139-69 as a head coach.

Throughout his career, Dungy was known for his commitment to faith, family, and community, was involved in charitable organizations such as the Fellowship of Christian Athletes, and authored books on leadership and character development.

Dungy's example serves as a reminder of the importance of hard work, perseverance, and a commitment to faith and values in achieving success both on and off the field. His dedication to respect, kindness, and leadership continues to inspire many, and his legacy lives on as a testament to the power of these qualities in building successful teams and communities.

An Inspiring Tale of Leadership and Respect

"Respect is not the size of your paycheck. It's the function of how you treat people." - Barbara Hall

John Maxwell, a renowned leadership expert and author, has gained immense respect from followers due to his impactful insights and genuine leadership style. One of the stories that exemplifies his ability to gain respect revolves around his interactions with his team during a challenging time.

In the early days of his leadership career, John Maxwell was tasked with turning around a struggling organization. The company was facing financial difficulties, low employee morale, and an overall sense of disillusionment. Maxwell knew that he had to not only implement effective strategies but also earn the respect and trust of his team to lead them through the transformation.

Rather than imposing his ideas from the top down, Maxwell took a different approach. He started by actively listening to his team members' concerns, ideas, and suggestions. He held open forums and encouraged open dialogue where employees felt heard and valued. Through this process, he not only gained a deep understanding of the challenges but also fostered an environment of collaboration and shared ownership.

Maxwell then began implementing changes based on the feedback he received. He involved team members in decision-making processes and acknowledged their contributions. His humility in admitting that he didn't have all the answers and his willingness to learn from his team members earned him their respect and loyalty.

As the organization started to improve under Maxwell's leadership, the respect he had earned from his team translated into increased productivity, engagement, and morale. His approach of valuing his team's input and creating a culture of collaboration not only turned the company around but also positioned Maxwell as a respected leader in the field of leadership development.

John Maxwell's story highlights the importance of actively listening, valuing team members, and being willing to learn from them. His genuine leadership style and commitment to empowering others earned him the respect of his followers and solidified his reputation as a trusted authority on leadership.

Applying Respect

"Leaders who win the respect of others are the ones who deliver more than they promise, not the ones who promise more than they can deliver." - Mark A. Clement

1. What qualities did Coach Dungy and John Maxwell possess that made them respected leaders?

_____

_____

_____

2. What can we learn from these stories about building trust and respect in our own lives and leadership styles?

_____

_____

_____

3. How can we encourage more individuals to act with empathy, honesty, accountability, respect, and integrity like the individuals in these stories?

_____

_____

_____

4. What impact do you think these stories can have on our own behavior and actions? How can we use them as examples to guide our own actions in our daily lives?

_____

_____

_____

5. Can you think of any other examples of leaders who have earned respect from their followers? What qualities did they possess that made them respected leaders?

_____

_____

_____

Unit 3
The Power of Integrity

"Leadership is about making others better as a result of your presence and making sure that impact lasts in your absence."
- Sheryl Sandberg

In a world that can often feel chaotic and unpredictable, integrity can be a superpower that sets leaders apart. The ability to act with honesty, transparency, and ethical fortitude can inspire trust and respect while fostering an environment of accountability and exacting standards.

In this Unit, we will examine the significance of integrity in leadership and explore ways to cultivate and enhance it. We will delve into the obstacles and potential pitfalls that leaders might encounter as they strive to embody integrity, as well as the valuable outcomes that stem from remaining steadfast in one's principles and values.

By sharing real-life stories, offering practical techniques, and providing thought-provoking exercises, we will assist readers in uncovering their own unique strength of integrity and its transformative influence across their leadership journey and everyday life.

Attributes of Integrity

"The supreme quality for leadership is unquestionably integrity. Without it, no real success is possible, no matter whether it is on a section gang, a football field, in an army, or in an office."
- Dwight D. Eisenhower

Keep promises: A leader who keeps his or her promises demonstrates integrity by showing that they can be trusted to follow through on their commitments. This can include promises to employees, customers, or stakeholders.

Admit mistakes: A leader who admits mistakes and takes responsibility for them demonstrates integrity by showing that he or she is accountable for their actions. This can include apologizing when mistakes are made and taking steps to rectify them.

Be transparent: A leader who is transparent in their actions and decisions demonstrates integrity by showing that they have nothing to hide. This can include sharing information with employees or stakeholders and being open to feedback and criticism.

Treat others fairly: A leader who treats others fairly and consistently demonstrates integrity by showing that they value fairness and equality. This can include treating all employees equally, regardless of their background or status.

Do what is right: A leader who does what is right, even when it is difficult or unpopular, demonstrates integrity by showing that they have a strong moral compass. This can include standing up for what is right, even if it means going against the norm or challenging authority.

Lead by example: A leader who sets a positive example for others to follow demonstrates integrity by showing that he or she practices what he or she preaches. This can include demonstrating excellent work ethics, respect, and responsibility.

Demonstrating Integrity

"Integrity is the essence of everything successful."
- R. Buckminster Fuller

1. Can you think of a time when you faced a difficult ethical decision? How did you approach the situation, and what did you learn from the experience?

_____

_____

_____

2. Have you ever made a mistake that went against your values? How did you rectify the situation, and what did you learn from the experience?

_____

_____

_____

3. Can you describe a time when you had to stand up for what was right, even when it was difficult or unpopular? How did you approach the situation, and what impact did your actions have?

_____

_____

_____

4. Have you ever faced pressure to compromise your integrity to achieve a goal? How did you handle the situation, and what did you learn from the experience?

_____

_____

_____

5. Can you think of a leader or mentor who demonstrated integrity? What qualities did they exhibit, and how did their integrity impact their leadership style and the culture of their organization?

_____

_____

_____

6. Have you ever encountered a situation where someone showed integrity towards you? How did it make you feel, and what impact did their actions have on your relationship with them?

_____

_____

_____

7. Can you think of a time when you had to make a tough decision that went against the interests of your organization or team? How did you approach the situation, and what impact did your decision have on the situation?

_____

_____

_____

A Woman of Integrity

"Integrity is telling myself the truth. And honesty is telling the truth to other people." - Spencer Johnson

Ruth Bader Ginsburg, a remarkable figure in American history, exemplified the power of integrity throughout her illustrious career as a lawyer and jurist. Her unwavering commitment to justice and her steadfast adherence to her principles made her a symbol of integrity and a champion for equality.

One of the defining moments that showcased Ginsburg's integrity was her dissenting opinion in the Supreme Court case of Ledbetter v. Goodyear Tire & Rubber Co. In this case, Lilly Ledbetter, a Goodyear employee, filed a lawsuit alleging pay discrimination based on gender. The majority of the court ruled against Ledbetter, stating that she had not filed her complaint within the required timeframe.

However, Ginsburg, in her powerful dissent, argued that the majority's decision was fundamentally flawed and unfair. She advocated for a broader interpretation of the law to protect workers from pay discrimination, emphasizing the importance of looking beyond technicalities and focusing on the underlying issue of gender inequality in the workplace. Ginsburg's passionate defense of justice and equality in the face of opposition highlighted her unwavering commitment to integrity.

Ginsburg's unwavering dedication to her principles, her fearless pursuit of justice, and her commitment to protecting the rights of all individuals, regardless of their gender, race, or background, demonstrated the immense power of integrity in leadership. She showed that by staying true to one's values and standing up for what is right, it is possible to make a lasting impact and create a more just and equitable society.

Ruth Bader Ginsburg's legacy serves as an inspiration to leaders across the world, reminding us of the transformative power of integrity and the importance of upholding principles of justice and equality.

The Integrity of a Champion

"Integrity is doing the right thing, even when no one is watching." - C. S. Lewis

Nick Foles is a remarkable example of a leader who embodies integrity both on and off the field. In the realm of sports, integrity often goes hand in hand with fair play and sportsmanship. Foles, the quarterback for the Philadelphia Eagles, demonstrated this quality in a profound way during Super Bowl LII in 2018.

In a dramatic and closely contested championship game, Foles led the Eagles against the New England Patriots. The game was a rollercoaster of emotions, with both teams battling fiercely for victory. In a pivotal moment, Foles found himself with an opportunity to make a historic play – a trick play that required him to catch a pass.

The play, now famously known as the "Philly Special," involved Foles lining up as a receiver and the ball being snapped to a running back, who then passed it to a third player, who was a tight end. The trick play worked to perfection, resulting in a touchdown for the Eagles. Foles caught the pass in the end zone, contributing to his team's success.

What stands out in this story is not just the success of the play but Foles' integrity throughout the process. He embraced his role as a receiver with the same dedication and enthusiasm as he did when he was the quarterback. Despite being a star player, he put the team's success above his individual glory. Foles' integrity shone brightly through his selflessness and commitment to the team's victory.

This story of Nick Foles demonstrates that integrity isn't just about being honest or having strong moral principles – it's about staying true to one's values, even in high-stakes situations. Foles' willingness to step into an unconventional role for the good of the team showcased his integrity and earned him the respect of teammates, fans, and the sports world at large.

Applying Integrity

"Integrity is the most valuable and respected quality of leadership. Always keep your word." - Brian Tracy

1. Ruth Bader Ginsburg showed unwavering integrity by standing up for what she believed, even in the face of opposition. Can you recall a situation in your leadership journey where you had to make a principled stand, and how did it impact your team or organization?

_____

_____

_____

2. Both stories emphasize the importance of integrity in upholding justice and fairness. Can you provide an example from your leadership experience where maintaining integrity was crucial in ensuring a just outcome?

_____

_____

_____

3. Integrity is closely linked to trust and credibility. Share an example of how your commitment to integrity has helped you gain the trust of your team members or colleagues?

_____

_____

_____

4. Can you think of a time when you or someone you know demonstrated integrity in a difficult situation?

_____

_____

_____

5. Share a personal story of how someone's integrity, whether a colleague, mentor, or team member, has influenced your own commitment to maintaining high ethical standards in your leadership role?

_____

_____

_____

Unit 4
The Power of Empathy

"Empathy is seeing with the eyes of another, listening with the ears of another, and feeling with the heart of another." - Alfred Adler

Empathy is an essential quality of great leaders. It is the ability to understand and relate to the emotions, thoughts, and experiences of others. Empathy is not just about being kind or compassionate; it is about being able to put yourself in someone else's shoes, to see the world from their perspective, and to genuinely care about their well-being.

Leaders who demonstrate empathy create an environment of trust, understanding, and connection. They listen attentively to their team members, take the time to understand their concerns, and show genuine care for their personal and professional development. They can anticipate others' needs and respond with sensitivity and compassion.

Empathy is particularly important in times of crisis or uncertainty. When people are facing challenging situations or experiencing difficult emotions, they need leaders who can provide comfort, support, and understanding. Empathetic leaders are able to connect with their team members on a deep level, providing reassurance and guidance during difficult times.

In this Unit, we will explore the power of empathy in leadership. We will discuss the benefits of cultivating empathy as a leader, share real-life examples of empathetic leadership, and provide practical tips for developing empathy in yourself and your team.

Whether you are a seasoned executive or a new manager, empathy is a skill that can be learned and cultivated, and it is essential for building strong, healthy, and productive relationships with your team members.

Attributes of Empathy

"The best leaders have a high degree of emotional intelligence. This means they have the ability to understand and manage their own emotions, as well as understand and relate to the emotions of others." - Daniel Goleman

Active Listening: A leader who actively listens to their team members demonstrates empathy by showing that they value their opinions and experiences. This can include asking open-ended questions, summarizing what the other person has said, and providing opportunities for feedback.

Understanding different perspectives: A leader who takes the time to understand different perspectives and experiences demonstrates empathy by showing that they value diversity and inclusivity. This can include seeking out different viewpoints, being open to feedback and criticism, and creating an environment where everyone feels valued and respected.

Communication: Clear and open communication can help foster empathy by creating an environment where everyone feels heard and understood.

Supporting work-life balance: A leader who supports work-life balance for their team members demonstrates empathy by recognizing the importance of personal well-being and mental health. This can include offering flexible schedules, encouraging breaks and time off, and promoting healthy habits and self-care.

Providing emotional support: A leader who provides emotional support to team members demonstrates empathy by showing that they care about their well-being and are willing to help when needed. This can include offering resources for mental health support, creating a safe and supportive work environment, and being available to listen and offer advice.

Collaborative Problem-Solving: Working collaboratively with team members to find solutions to problems can help foster a sense of empathy and support within the team.

Personal Connection: Taking the time to connect with team members on a personal level can help build trust and foster empathy.

Celebrating successes: A leader who celebrates the successes of team members demonstrates empathy by showing that they appreciate and value their contributions. This can include recognizing accomplishments, offering praise and rewards, and creating a positive and supportive work culture.

Flexibility: Being flexible and accommodating can show empathy by recognizing and responding to the needs of team members.

Demonstrating Empathy

"A leader without empathy is like a doctor without bedside manners. They may have the knowledge and skill, but they won't be able to truly connect with their patients." - Unknown

1. Can you think of a time when you demonstrated empathy towards a team member? What did you do, and what impact did it have on the situation?

_____

_____

_____

2. How do you ensure that you are considering the needs and perspectives of others in your decision-making process?

_____

_____

_____

3. How can a leader support work-life balance for their team members, and how does this demonstrate empathy?

_____

_____

_____

4. Can you describe a time when you had to manage a team member's emotions or help them navigate a difficult situation? How did you approach the situation, and what impact did your actions have?

_____

_____

_____

5. How can empathy be incorporated into leadership development and training programs?

_____

_____

_____

Compassionate Leadership

"Leadership is about empathy. It is about having the ability to relate to and connect with people for the purpose of inspiring and empowering their lives." - Oprah Winfrey

Howard Schultz is the former CEO of Starbucks. In 2008, Starbucks faced a major financial crisis, which led to the closure of hundreds of stores and thousands of job losses. In response, Schultz took a bold and empathetic approach by launching a program called "Leadership Lab," where he invited 10,000 store managers to Seattle to discuss the company's future.

During the program, Schultz shared his own personal story of growing up in a poor family and how he understood the fear and uncertainty that many employees were feeling during this time of crisis. He also encouraged employees to speak openly about their concerns and ideas for the company's future.

Through his empathy and open communication, Schultz created a sense of unity and purpose among Starbucks employees, which helped the company recover and thrive in the years after the crisis. This story illustrates the power of empathy in leadership and how it can help to build trust, inspire collaboration, and drive positive change.

The Empathy of a Leader

"The ability to put yourself in someone else's shoes is a key leadership skill. It's how we build the trust that makes leadership possible." - Seth Godin

In 2009, while working in the Private Banking Division in Atlanta, my family was going through a tough time. My sister-in-law had been diagnosed with stage 4 colon cancer and was living with us while undergoing chemotherapy and managing her illness. Christmas was approaching, and we knew it would be her last holiday with us. She was given only months to live, and we wanted to make this an incredibly special time.

Balancing work and family responsibilities became overwhelming, and I was starting to arrive late to meetings. I knew it was affecting my work performance and decided to confide in my manager.

I entered his office, took a deep breath, and explained our situation. To my surprise, he shared his own similar experience and expressed his condolences. He looked at his watch and said, "You are on family leave as of now, and don't worry about returning until you are ready." The office will take care of everything while you are gone.

I was filled with relief and gratitude, never expecting someone in a leadership position to show such empathy and understanding. I was able to take time off to be with my family during this challenging time and returned to work with a newfound respect for my manager. This experience taught me the importance of leaders showing empathy and the impact it can have on their employees.

Applying Empathy

"Empathy is about standing in someone else's shoes, feeling with his or her heart, seeing with his or her eyes." - Daniel H. Pink

1. Have you ever encountered a situation where someone showed empathy towards you? How did it make you feel, and what impact did their actions have on your relationship with them?

_____

_____

_____

2. Can you think of a leader or mentor who demonstrated empathy? What qualities did they exhibit, and how did their empathy impact their leadership style and the culture of their organization?

_____

_____

_____

3. In what ways can leaders demonstrate empathy in their interactions with customers and team members?

_____

_____

_____

4. What can you learn from these stories about empathy, and how can you apply it in your own leadership roles?

_____

_____

_____

Unit 5
The Power of Humility

"To lead the people, walk behind them." - Lao Tzu

Humility is a quality that is often overlooked in our society. In a world where success is often measured by wealth, power, and fame, it can be easy to forget the value of humility. Yet, some of the greatest leaders in history have shown the power of humility in their actions and words. From Mahatma Gandhi to Mother Teresa, from Nelson Mandela to Martin Luther King Jr., leaders who have shown humility have had a profound impact on their followers and the world.

Humility is not about being weak or submissive; rather, it is about recognizing the limits of our knowledge and abilities and having the courage to admit when we are wrong. A humble leader is willing to listen to the opinions of others, learn from his or her mistakes, and share the credit for their successes. They are not threatened by the strengths of others but rather seek to bring out the best in everyone around them.

In this Unit, we will explore the power of humility in leadership. We will examine how humility can inspire trust, promote collaboration, and lead to more effective decision-making. We will look at real-life examples of humble leaders and the impact they have had on their followers and organizations. Finally, we will discuss practical strategies for developing humility as a leader and using it to enhance your leadership abilities.

Attributes of Humility

"Humility is the courage to be honest with ourselves and to others, regardless of the cost." - Unknown

Acknowledge mistakes: Take responsibility for mistakes and seek to learn from them. Admit when you do not know something; a leader is not afraid to admit when they do not know something and seeks to learn from others.

Share credit with others: Recognize the contributions of team members and share credit for successes.

Seek feedback: Actively seek feedback from team members and be open to constructive criticism.

Listen actively: Listen actively to team members, seeking to understand their perspectives and experiences.

Value others' opinions: Value the opinions and experiences of others and seek to create an inclusive environment where everyone feels heard and valued.

Serve others: A leader prioritizes the needs of their team members and seeks to serve them.

Be willing to learn and grow: Leaders recognize that they have room for growth and are willing to learn from others and continue developing their skills and knowledge.

Demonstrating Humility

"The greatest leaders are willing to admit their mistakes, and they learn from them." - John C. Maxwell

1. Can you think of a leader who has demonstrated humility? How did they accomplish this?

_____

_____

_____

2. What are some benefits of a leader demonstrating humility in the workplace?

_____

_____

_____

3. Why do you think it can be difficult for leaders to show humility?

_____

_____

_____

4. Have you ever worked for a leader who lacked humility? How did this impact the work environment?

_____

_____

_____

5. How can leaders strike a balance between showing confidence and demonstrating humility?

_____

_____

_____

6. Can you think of any situations in which a leader might need to put their own ego aside for the good of the team or organization?

_____

_____

_____

7. What are some ways a leader can cultivate a culture of humility within their team or organization?

_____

_____

_____

8. How can a leader's humility inspire and motivate their team members?

_____

_____

_____

9. What are some common misconceptions about humility in leadership?

_____

_____

_____

10. In what ways can a leader's humility contribute to the success of a project or organization?

_____

_____

_____

Leading with Humility

"The most successful leaders are those who are humble enough to recognize their own limitations and seek out the advice and expertise of others." - Unknown

Satya Nadella is a well-known business executive who has been CEO of Microsoft Corporation since 2014. However, what many people may not know about Nadella is the story of his rise to leadership, which is marked by an intense sense of humility.

Nadella was born in India and moved to the United States to pursue his graduate studies. He joined Microsoft in 1992 and quickly rose through the ranks to become the president of the Server and Tools division in 2011. When he was selected to become the CEO of Microsoft in 2014, he faced a daunting challenge. The company was struggling to compete with rivals such as Google and Apple, and many analysts were skeptical about its future.

One of the first things that Nadella did as CEO was to emphasize the importance of empathy and humility in leadership. He recognized that Microsoft had become too focused on its own internal goals and needed to reconnect with its customers and the broader community. To achieve this, he launched a program called "One Microsoft," which aimed to break down the silos between different departments and create a more cohesive company culture.

Nadella also encouraged his team to take risks and be open to failure. He believed that innovation required a willingness to experiment and learn from mistakes, and he demonstrated this by sharing his own failures and mistakes with his colleagues.

The most striking example of Nadella's humility came in 2018 when he admitted that Microsoft had been wrong to treat open-source software as a threat. He said that he had come to realize that open-source technology was a valuable resource that could help Microsoft build better products and services. This was a major shift in the company's strategy, and it demonstrated Nadella's willingness to learn from others and put the needs of the company ahead of his own ego.

Today, Microsoft is thriving under Nadella's leadership. The company has regained its position as a major player in the tech industry, and it is widely admired for its innovative products and services. Nadella's emphasis on empathy and humility has been a key factor in this success, and it serves as a powerful reminder of the importance of these qualities in leadership.

An Inspiring Tale of Humility

"Humility is not weakness, but it's opposite. It is a willingness to surrender pride and open oneself to the possibility of learning and growth." - Unknown

In 2018, a high school basketball coach named Steve Belcher made headlines for his act of humility during a game. Belcher's team, the Olivet Eagles, was facing off against the opposing team, the Lansing Christian Pilgrims. The Eagles had just won the game when Belcher noticed something strange happening on the court.

One of the opposing players, Grant Spicer, was sitting on the bench, crying. Belcher went over to talk to him and found out that Spicer had accidentally tipped the ball into the Eagles' basket during the game-winning shot. Spicer was devastated, thinking that he had cost his team the win.

Belcher knew this was not the case and decided to act. He asked the referees if they could review the game-winning shot, and they agreed. Upon reviewing the footage, they determined that the shot was indeed scored by one of the Eagles members and not the Pilgrims' Spicer Belcher then went over to Spicer and told him the good news.

This act of humility by Belcher was praised by many, including the opposing coach and the referees. It demonstrated that Belcher cared more about doing the right thing than about winning at all costs. His actions also showed his players that integrity and sportsmanship were more important than any win or loss.

This story reminds us that humility is not just about being modest or self-effacing; it is also about putting others before ourselves and doing what is right, even when it is hard or goes against our interests.

Applying Humility

"No man will make a great leader who wants to do it all himself, or to get all the credit for doing it." - Andrew Carnegie.

1. Reflecting on the stories, how can leaders balance humility with confidence and decisiveness in their decision-making processes?

_____

_____

_____

2. In what ways have you seen the virtue of humility positively impact leadership dynamics, both in your own experiences and in the stories we explored?

_____

_____

_____

3. How can leaders use humility to create a more positive and collaborative work environment?

_____

_____

_____

4. In what ways can a leader's humble approach to leadership benefit the overall success of an organization?

_____

_____

_____

5. How can we develop and cultivate humility as a leadership trait, and why is it important to do so?

_____

_____

_____

Unit 6
The Power of Courage

"Leadership requires the courage to make decisions that will benefit the next generation." - Alan Autry

Leadership requires courage. Whether it is making complex decisions, taking calculated risks, or speaking up for what is right, courage is a defining trait of effective leaders. It takes courage to face uncertainty and to take action in the face of adversity. Leaders who possess this quality are not only able to inspire their team members but also to make a positive impact on the world around them.

At the heart of courage is vulnerability, which requires a willingness to take risks and to be open to the possibility of failure. It requires stepping out of one's comfort zone and embracing the unknown. However, it is important to note that courage is not the absence of fear but the willingness to act despite it. It takes courage to face our fears and push beyond our limitations.

Leaders who possess courage are not afraid to take on challenges and pursue their goals with determination and conviction. They are willing to stand up for their beliefs and take responsibility for their actions. They can inspire and motivate others to be their best selves, even in adversity.

In this Unit, we will explore the power of courage in leadership, examining how it can inspire others, lead to positive change, and help leaders overcome obstacles. We will look at the characteristics of courageous leaders, the benefits of courage in the workplace, and examples of leaders who have demonstrated this quality in action. Through this exploration, we hope to inspire and encourage leaders to embrace their own courage and lead with conviction and purpose.

Attributes of Courage

"The ultimate measure of a man is not where he stands in moments of comfort and convenience, but where he stands at times of challenge and controversy." - Martin Luther King Jr.

Stand up for what is right: Leaders who show courage are willing to speak up and stand up for what is right, even if it means going against the majority or the status quo.

Take risks: Leaders are willing to take calculated risks and embrace uncertainty in pursuit of their goals. They are not afraid to step out of their comfort zones and try new things.

Admit mistakes: Leaders admit when they are wrong and take responsibility for their mistakes. They use these moments as opportunities to learn and grow and do not let their ego get in the way of doing what is right.

Resilience: Leaders are resilient in the face of adversity. They do not give up easily and are willing to persevere through tough times to achieve goals.

Empower others: Leaders empower others to be courageous as well. They create a culture of trust and support where team members feel safe to take risks and speak up.

Innovation: Leaders are willing to challenge the status quo and push the boundaries of what is possible. They encourage team members to think outside the box and produce creative solutions to problems.

Visionary thinking: Leaders have a strong vision for the future and are willing to take bold steps to make it a reality. They inspire their team members to believe in their vision and work towards a common goal.

Demonstrating Courage

"Courage is what it takes to stand up and speak. Courage is also what it takes to sit down and listen." - Winston Churchill

1. Can you provide an example of a leader who showed courage in a difficult situation? How did their actions impact the outcome?

_____

_____

_____

2. What are some common fears that leaders face in their roles? How can they overcome these fears to demonstrate courage?

_____

_____

_____

3. How does courage in leadership relate to making tough decisions? Can you give an example of a leader who made a tough decision that required courage?

_____

_____

_____

4. What role does vulnerability play in leadership courage? Can a leader be courageous while still being vulnerable?

_____

_____

_____

5. How can leaders inspire courage in their team members? Can you think of a time when a leader motivated you to take courageous action?

_____

_____

_____

Overcoming Adversity with Courage

"Courage is not the absence of fear, but the triumph over it."
- Nelson Mandela

Wilma Rudolph was an American track and field athlete who overcame many obstacles and displayed immense courage throughout her career. Born prematurely, she suffered from polio at the age of four, which left her with a twisted leg and foot. She also had scarlet fever and pneumonia, and her doctors feared she might never walk again.

Despite her physical disabilities, Rudolph refused to let them stop her from pursuing her passion for running. She began training under her high school coach, who recognized her potential and helped her hone her skills. Rudolph's talent became apparent when she won a bronze medal at the 1956 Olympics at sixteen. However, it was the 1960 Olympics in Rome that cemented her status as a legend.

At the Rome Olympics, Rudolph became the first American woman to win three gold medals in a single Olympiad. She won the 100-meter dash, the 200-meter dash, and the 4x100-meter relay. Rudolph's victories were even more impressive because she had to overcome racial discrimination, which was still prevalent at the time. She faced insults, heckling, and segregation, but she refused to let them distract her from her goal.

Rudolph's achievements at the Olympics earned her widespread acclaim, and she became a symbol of hope and courage for millions of people around the world. She later retired from competition and dedicated her life to helping disadvantaged children. Rudolph's legacy as an athlete and a humanitarian endures to this day, inspiring generations of people to overcome their own obstacles with courage and determination.

Courageous Leadership

"It takes courage to lead. Courage to make tough decisions. Courage to stand up for what is right, even when others disagree. Courage to keep going when the going gets tough." - Unknown

Jourdan Bender was just sixteen years old when Hurricane Katrina hit New Orleans in 2005. Like many residents of the city, Jourdan and her family were displaced from their homes and had to evacuate to safety. When they returned, they found that their community had been devastated by the hurricane.

Despite the challenges she faced, Jourdan was determined to make a difference and help her community recover. Along with a group of other young people, she formed the Young People's Project (YPP) to organize community meetings and identify areas of need.

One of the projects that Jourdan and the YPP took on was the rebuilding of a public library in the Lower Ninth Ward, one of the hardest-hit areas of the city. The library had been destroyed by the hurricane, and Jourdan saw it as a critical resource for the community.

Jourdan and the YPP worked tirelessly to raise funds, gather materials, and recruit volunteers to help with the rebuilding effort. They faced numerous obstacles along the way, including a lack of funding, bureaucratic red tape, and safety concerns. But Jourdan and her team never gave up.

Despite the dangers and difficulties of working in a disaster zone, Jourdan remained committed to her goal. She worked long hours alongside other volunteers, often in hazardous conditions, to rebuild the library and other community facilities.

Through their efforts, Jourdan and the YPP helped to bring hope and healing to the people of New Orleans. They showed that even young people can make a significant impact on their communities when they work together and stay committed to their goals. Their example inspired many others to get involved in the rebuilding effort and demonstrated the power of ordinary people to create positive change in the face of adversity.

Jourdan's leadership and courage in the aftermath of Hurricane Katrina showed that even in the most challenging circumstances, people could come together to make a difference and create a brighter future for their community.

Applying Courage

"It takes courage to lead, to step up and take charge even when faced with uncertainty." - John C. Maxwell

1. In what ways have you personally witnessed or experienced acts of courage in leadership similar to the stories discussed?

_____

_____

_____

2. Reflecting on the stories, how does courage complement and enhance effective leadership? Can you share an example from your own leadership journey?

_____

_____

_____

3. Reflect on a time in your own life when you had to demonstrate courage to overcome a challenge or achieve a goal. How did you approach the situation, and what were the outcomes?

_____

_____

_____

4. How can leaders cultivate courage within themselves and their teams to navigate difficult situations and make impactful decisions?

_____

_____

_____

5. In what ways can leaders foster a culture of courage within their organizations, encouraging team members to take risks and pursue innovative solutions?

_____

_____

_____

Unit 7
The Power of Resilience

"True leaders are not those who never fail, but those who know how to rise up from their failures with resilience and determination." - Unknown

Resilience is the ability to bounce back from adversity to weather the storms of life and come out stronger on the other side. It is essential in navigating the difficulties of life, especially in leadership roles. Leaders with resilience can persevere in the face of challenges and setbacks, maintain a positive outlook, and inspire their teams to do the same.

Resilience is not a trait that one is born with; it is a skill that can be developed and strengthened over time. It requires a mindset that embraces challenges as opportunities for growth and learning and an unwavering determination to keep moving forward, even in the face of obstacles.

In this Unit, we will explore the power of resilience in leadership and how it can be cultivated and harnessed to achieve success in both personal and professional endeavors. We will examine the traits and characteristics of resilient leaders, the strategies and tools they use to build and maintain resilience, and the impact that resilience has on their teams and organizations.

Through inspiring stories and practical advice, we will learn how to develop a resilient mindset, embrace change and uncertainty, and overcome adversity with grace and fortitude. We will discover that resilience is not only a key to success but also a fundamental element of a fulfilling and meaningful life.

Let's explore the transformative power of resilience and how it can help us overcome any challenge and achieve our goals and dreams.

Attributes of Resilience

"Leadership is about resilience and perseverance. It's about being able to face adversity head-on and come out stronger on the other side." - Indra Nooyi

Adaptability: Resilient leaders are adaptable and flexible. They can adjust their plans and strategies in response to changing circumstances and are not afraid to take risks or try new things.

Positive attitude: Resilient leaders maintain a positive attitude even in the face of setbacks and challenges. They focus on finding solutions rather than dwelling on problems, and they can inspire and motivate their team to keep moving forward.

Perseverance: Resilient leaders are persistent and determined. They don't give up easily, and they are willing to work hard to achieve their goals, even in the face of obstacles and setbacks.

Emotional intelligence: Resilient leaders have strong emotional intelligence. They can manage their own emotions effectively, and they are empathetic and supportive of others, which helps them to build strong relationships and trust.

Self-awareness: Resilient leaders are self-aware and able to recognize their own strengths and weaknesses. They are open to feedback and willing to learn and grow, which enables them to adapt and improve their performance.

Strategic thinking: Resilient leaders are strategic thinkers. They can anticipate and plan for potential challenges and have an unclouded vision and plan for achieving their goals.

Effective communication skills: Resilient leaders have effective communication skills. They can articulate their vision and goals clearly and effectively and inspire and motivate their teams through effective communication.

Demonstrating Resilience

"Leadership requires resilience - the ability to keep going in the face of setbacks, obstacles, and challenges." - Richard Branson

1. What are some common challenges that leaders face, and how can resilience help them overcome these challenges?

_____

_____

_____

2. How can leaders develop resilience, and what practices can they adopt to cultivate this trait?

_____

_____

_____

3. What are some specific examples of leaders who have shown resilience in the face of adversity, and what can we learn from their experiences?

_____

_____

_____

4. How can a leader's resilience positively impact their team or organization, and why is this trait so important in leadership?

_____

_____

_____

5. How does resilience intersect with other leadership traits, such as adaptability, emotional intelligence, and determination?

_____

_____

_____

The Resilient Leader Who Transformed an Industry

"Resilience is knowing that you are the only one that has the power and the responsibility to pick yourself up." - Mary Holloway

Steve Jobs, the co-founder and CEO of Apple Inc., is widely regarded as one of the most innovative and successful entrepreneurs of the modern era. However, his path to success was not without its setbacks and challenges.

In 1985, Steve Jobs was forced out of Apple, the company he helped create, after a power struggle with the board of directors. Devastated and humiliated, he left the company and went on to start NeXT Computer, a new computer company. Despite his earlier success with Apple, NeXT initially struggled to gain traction in the marketplace, with few customers willing to invest in expensive hardware and software.

Despite these setbacks, Jobs remained flexible and determined to succeed. He continued to innovate and develop new technologies, eventually creating the NeXTSTEP operating system, which was widely praised for its advanced features and performance. In 1996, Apple purchased NeXT Computer for $429 million, bringing Jobs back into the company he helped create.

Upon his return to Apple, Jobs was determined to turn the company around and restore it to its former glory. He oversaw the development of new products, including the iMac, iPod, iPhone, and iPad, which revolutionized the computer, music, and mobile phone industries.

Despite his many successes, Jobs faced numerous setbacks and challenges throughout his career, including health issues that eventually led to his death in 2011. However, his resilience and determination to succeed helped him overcome these obstacles and achieve greatness.

Steve Jobs' story is a powerful example of the importance of resilience in leadership. His ability to bounce back from setbacks and continue pursuing his goals is a testament to the power of perseverance and determination.

From Adversity to Triumph: The Power of Resilience

"Success is not final, failure is not fatal: It is the courage to continue that counts."
- Winston Churchill

J. K. Rowling is a well-known author, best known for writing the Harry Potter series of books. However, before she became a successful author, she faced numerous challenges and setbacks that tested her resilience.

Rowling's journey to becoming an author was not an easy one. In her mid-twenties, she was living in poverty, going through a divorce, and raising a young child on her own. Despite these challenges, she continued to work on her writing and submitted her manuscript to several publishers. However, she was rejected by every one of them.

Despite the rejections, Rowling refused to give up on her dream of becoming a published author. She kept working on her manuscript and sent it out to more publishers. Finally, after many attempts, she received an offer from Bloomsbury, a small publishing company in the UK.

After signing a contract with Bloomsbury, Rowling's first book in the Harry Potter series was published in 1997. The book was an instant success, winning numerous awards and sparking a global phenomenon. Despite her incredible success, Rowling continued to face challenges in her personal life. She lost her mother to multiple sclerosis and later suffered from depression and suicidal thoughts. However, she used her own experiences to inspire her writing, and her characters often faced similar struggles.

Through her journey, Rowling demonstrated incredible resilience and determination. Despite facing numerous setbacks, she refused to give up on her dream and kept working towards it. Her story is a testament to the power of resilience in overcoming obstacles and achieving success.

Applying Resilience

"Resilience is not about being able to bounce back immediately; it's about persevering in the face of setbacks and failures."
- Sheryl Sandberg

1. What challenges have you faced in your life, and how have you overcome them?

_____

_____

_____

2. How do you handle failure and setbacks, and what strategies do you use to bounce back?

_____

_____

_____

3. How do you cope with stress and adversity, and what techniques have worked for you in the past?

_____

_____

_____

4. What are your core values and beliefs, and how do they shape your approach to resilience?

_____

_____

_____

5. How do you cultivate a growth mindset and learn from difficult experiences?

_____

_____

_____

6. How can you apply the lessons of Steve Jobs and J. K. Rowling to your own life and leadership journey?

_____

_____

_____

7. How can you foster resilience in others and create a supportive, empowering environment for growth and development?

_____

_____

_____

Unit 8
Empowerment

"Empowerment is not giving people power, it's releasing the power they already have." - John Stahl-Wert

Leadership is not just about directing others, but it also requires self-awareness and strength. It takes a confident and inspired individual to lead others effectively. Empowerment involves having the courage and confidence to take risks, challenge the status quo, and make decisions. In today's world, leadership and encouragement go hand in hand.

Empowerment is not something that is given to you, but rather, it is something that you must take for yourself. It requires a mindset of growth and a willingness to learn, adapt, and take on new challenges. Empowering yourself involves building your self-awareness, identifying your strengths and weaknesses, and taking ownership of your career development. It also involves developing a growth mindset and continuously seeking new learning opportunities to enhance your skills and knowledge.

As you empower yourself, you will also become a more effective leader. You will be better equipped to inspire, motivate, and support your team to achieve their goals. Empowering leadership involves creating a positive work culture that encourages growth and development, recognizes achievements, and supports individuals through challenges.

In this Unit, we will explore the concept of empowerment in leadership and provide practical guidance on how to empower yourself as a leader. We will discuss the importance of self-awareness, the benefits of continuous learning, and the impact of a growth mindset. By the end of this Unit, you will have a deeper understanding of empowerment in leadership and the tools and strategies needed to become an empowering leader. Let's get started on your journey to self-empowerment and leadership!

Attributes of Empowerment

"If your actions inspire others to dream more, learn more, do more, and become more, you are a leader." - John Quincy Adams

Visionary: An empowering leader should have a clear vision and be able to communicate it effectively to the team.

Collaborative: Empowering Leaders should be willing to collaborate with their teams and value their input and ideas.

Transparent: An empowering leader should be open and transparent about his or her decisions and actions, fostering trust and accountability within the team.

Courageous: Empowering leaders take risks and make tough decisions, even in the face of uncertainty.

Supportive: An empowering leader provides support and guidance to the team, helping them overcome obstacles and achieve their goals.

Accountable: Empowering leaders hold themselves accountable for their actions and decisions and model accountability for their teams.

Resilient: An empowering leader bounces back from setbacks and failures and help their team do the same.

Inclusive: Empowering leaders embrace diversity and inclusivity and create a safe and inclusive environment for their team.

Adaptive: An empowering leader adapts to changing circumstances and pivots when necessary.

Inspirational: An empowering leader inspires and motivates the team, fostering a sense of purpose and passion among team members.

Demonstrating Empowerment

Leadership is about empowering people to make a positive difference in the world." - Richard Branson

1. How does empowerment impact the performance of employees in a team or organization?

_____

_____

_____

2. How can leaders effectively empower their team members to take ownership and responsibility for their work?

_____

_____

_____

3. What role does trust play in creating an empowered workplace culture?

_____

_____

_____

4. How can leaders strike a balance between empowering their team members and maintaining accountability and control?

_____

_____

_____

5. How can an empowered workplace culture lead to increased creativity and innovation?

_____

_____

_____

6. How does an empowered workplace culture affect employee retention and job satisfaction?

_____

_____

_____

7. How can leaders use feedback to empower their team members and foster a culture of continuous improvement?

_____

_____

_____

Empowering Leadership

"The best leader is the one who has sense enough to pick good men to do what he wants done, and self-restraint to keep from meddling with them while they do it." - Theodore Roosevelt

Indra Nooyi is a well-known Indian American business executive who served as the CEO of PepsiCo from 2006 to 2018. During her tenure, she transformed PepsiCo into a more health-oriented company by shifting the focus from sugary drinks to healthier options like water and juices.

One of the key aspects of Nooyi's leadership style was her emphasis on empowerment. She believed that empowering her employees was the key to driving innovation and growth within the company.

Nooyi's philosophy of empowerment was reflected in her decision-making processes. Rather than making decisions in a vacuum, she sought input from her team members and encouraged them to take ownership of their work. This approach not only led to better decisions but also fostered a culture of collaboration and accountability.

Nooyi's commitment to empowerment and diversity was also evident in her efforts to promote women to leadership positions. She recognized the importance of representation and actively worked to promote and mentor women within the company. Her efforts were recognized when she was named the third most powerful woman in business by *Fortune* magazine in 2014.

Overall, Indra Nooyi's leadership style exemplifies empowerment in driving innovation and growth within a company. Her focus on collaboration, diversity, and inclusivity led to a more engaged and motivated workforce, which led to the success of PepsiCo during her tenure.

Breaking Barriers: Journey to Empowerment

"Empowerment is the key to unlocking the potential of every individual and creating a better world for all." - Melinda Gates

Mary Barr is the CEO of General Motors (GM), the first female CEO of a major automaker in history. She has been with GM for over forty years and has held various positions throughout the company, including serving as the head of human resources, global product development, and supply chain.

One of the key aspects of Barra's leadership style is empowerment. She strongly believes in giving employees the tools and resources they need to succeed and fostering a culture of accountability and ownership. This philosophy was put to the test in 2014 when GM faced a major crisis involving a faulty ignition switch in some of their vehicles, which led to numerous accidents and fatalities.

Barra took swift and decisive action, leading the company's efforts to investigate and address the issue. She acknowledged the company's mistakes and apologized to those affected by the faulty switches, and she implemented significant changes to the company's internal processes and culture to prevent such a crisis from happening again.

One of the most notable changes she made was to create a new position of Vice President for Global Vehicle Safety, which reports directly to her. This move ensures that safety concerns are given top priority and the company is held accountable for any safety-related issues.

Barra's commitment to empowerment is evident in how she handled the crisis. She empowered her team to take ownership of the problem and find solutions, and she provided the resources and support needed to make that happen. She also empowered customers by creating a compensation fund for those affected by the faulty switches, showing that the company was taking responsibility for their mistakes.

Under Barra's leadership, GM has continued to make significant strides in innovation and sustainability, with a focus on electric and autonomous vehicles. She has also worked to create a more diverse and inclusive workforce, recognizing the value that different perspectives and backgrounds can bring to the table.

Barra's story is a powerful example of how empowerment can lead to success, even in the face of significant challenges. By giving employees the tools and resources they need to succeed and fostering a culture of accountability and ownership, Barra has been able to lead GM through one of its most difficult periods and position the company for continued success in the future.

Applying Empowerment

"Leadership is about making others better as a result of your presence and making sure that impact lasts in your absence."
- Sheryl Sandberg

1. What personal beliefs and values do you hold that align with the leadership styles of Mary Barra and Indra Nooyi?

_____

_____

_____

2. How can you incorporate the principles of empowerment into your own leadership style?

_____

_____

_____

3. What barriers do you face in implementing empowerment in your organization or team, and how can you overcome them?

_____

_____

_____

4. How can you actively work to create a culture of empowerment in your workplace or community?

_____

_____

_____

5. In what ways can you empower and support the growth and development of others, including your colleagues, subordinates, and mentees?

_____

_____

_____

6. How can you balance the need for empowerment with the need for accountability and results in your leadership role?

_____

_____

_____

7. How can you use your leadership position to create a positive social impact and empower others to do the same?

_____

_____

_____

8. What steps can you take to ensure that my leadership style is inclusive, ethical, and empowering for all individuals and communities?

_____

_____

_____

Unit 9
The Power of Communication

"The single biggest problem in communication is the illusion that it has taken place." - George Bernard Shaw

Leadership and communication are inseparable. Effective leaders understand that communication is a cornerstone of their success and that without clear and effective communication skills, their ability to lead will be diminished. Communication is the key to building trust, inspiring action, and achieving results.

In this Unit, we will explore the crucial relationship between leadership and communication and provide practical insights and strategies for enhancing communication skills as a leader.

We will examine the different types of communication, including verbal, nonverbal, and written, and explore the various channels of communication available to leaders. Additionally, we will discuss the importance of active listening, empathetic communication, and the role of feedback in effective communication. Whether you are leading a team or an entire organization, effective communication is essential to your success as a leader. Let's dive in and explore the fascinating and essential world of leadership and communication.

Attributes of Successful Communication

"Great leaders are willing to sacrifice their own personal interests for the good of the team. They understand that the true strength of any organization lies in the quality of its communication."
- John C. Maxwell

Clarity: Being clear in your communication is important for ensuring that your message is understood correctly. This means being concise and to the point, avoiding jargon and technical language that might confuse others.

Active listening: Effective communication is a two-way process, and active listening is a key part of this. Leaders who are good communicators actively listen to others, giving them their full attention and showing that they value their input.

Empathy: Empathy is an important aspect of communication, especially when it comes to understanding and responding to others' emotions. Leaders who show empathy are better able to build trust and understanding with their team members.

Confidence: Confidence in communication is important for conveying authority and credibility. Leaders who are confident in their communication are more likely to inspire confidence in others.

Flexibility: Effective communication requires flexibility and adaptability. Leaders who can adjust their communication style to fit the needs of different team members or situations are better able to build strong relationships and resolve conflicts.

Transparency: Transparency in communication is important for building trust and credibility with team members. Leaders who are open and honest in their communication are more likely to be seen as trustworthy and respected.

Feedback: Giving and receiving feedback is an important part of effective communication in leadership. Leaders open to receiving feedback and providing constructive feedback to their team members can help build a culture of growth and improvement within their organization.

Storytelling: Storytelling is a powerful way to communicate ideas and build connections with others. Leaders who are skilled at telling stories can inspire and motivate their team members, helping them to understand and connect with the organization's mission and values.

Demonstrating Effective Communication

"Effective communication is 20% what you know and 80% how you feel about what you know." - Jim Rohn

1. How can effective communication improve team collaboration and productivity?

_____

_____

_____

2. What are some strategies leaders can use to ensure they are communicating clearly and effectively with their team?

_____

_____

_____

3. How can leaders use communication to build trust and rapport with their team members?

_____

_____

_____

4. In what ways can leaders use communication to motivate and inspire their teams to achieve their goals?

_____

_____

_____

5. How can leaders effectively communicate difficult or sensitive information to their teams in a way that is respectful and empathetic?

_____

_____

_____

6. What role does active listening play in effective communication as a leader?

_____

_____

_____

7. How can leaders adapt their communication style to different team members or situations?

_____

_____

_____

8. How can nonverbal communication, such as body language and tone of voice, affect the effectiveness of a leader's message?

_____

_____

_____

9. What are some common communication mistakes that leaders should avoid?

_____

_____

_____

10. How can leaders use feedback and constructive criticism to improve their communication skills?

_____

_____

_____

Masterful Communication

"Communication is a skill that you can learn. It's like riding a bicycle or typing. If you're willing to work at it, you can rapidly improve the quality of every part of your life." - Brian Tracy

Winston Churchill, the former Prime Minister of the United Kingdom, was widely known for his exceptional communication skills. Churchill is often regarded as one of the greatest orators of the twentieth century due to his ability to inspire and motivate people through his speeches during some of the most challenging times in British history.

During World War II, Churchill gave a series of powerful speeches that helped rally the British people and boost morale during a time of great adversity. One of his most famous speeches, the "We Shall Fight on the Beaches" speech, was delivered in 1940 when Britain was facing the threat of a German invasion. In this speech, Churchill spoke with conviction and passion, urging the British people to stand firm in the face of danger and defend their country at all costs.

Churchill's ability to communicate effectively was also evident in his radio broadcasts, where he spoke directly to the people and provided updates on the war effort. His speeches were characterized by his use of simple, direct language and his ability to connect with his audience on an emotional level.

Overall, Churchill's communication skills played a crucial role in rallying the British people during World War II and inspiring them to persevere in the face of adversity. His legacy as a great communicator continues to inspire leaders worldwide.

The Communicator Who Broke Barriers

"Great leaders are willing to sacrifice their own personal interests for the good of the team. They communicate their intent clearly and effectively, and they inspire others to do the same."
- Simon Sinek

Ronald Reagan, the 40th President of the United States, is widely regarded as one of the most effective communicators in American political history. His leadership in communication was instrumental in shaping public opinion and advancing his policy agenda. Here's a story that illustrates Reagan's remarkable communication skills:

In the early 1980s, during Reagan's presidency, the United States faced a severe economic recession with high inflation and unemployment rates. The American people were anxious and looking for leadership to address these challenges.

Reagan understood the importance of clear and persuasive communication in times of crisis. He decided to directly address the nation in a televised speech from the Oval Office. On July 27, 1981, he delivered what came to be known as the "Reaganomics" speech, outlining his economic policies to revitalize the country.

During this speech, Reagan used simple and relatable language to explain his vision. He famously said, "In this present crisis, government is not the solution to our problem; government is the problem." This line succinctly conveyed his belief in limited government intervention in the economy and his commitment to free-market principles.

Reagan's communication style was marked by optimism, empathy, and a sense of conviction. He had the ability to connect with people on a personal level, making complex economic policies understandable and relatable. He spoke directly to the concerns of ordinary Americans, promising them a brighter future.

The "Reaganomics" speech was not just a one-time event. Reagan consistently communicated his economic vision through various speeches, press conferences, and public appearances. He employed memorable anecdotes and humor to engage his audience and drive home his points.

Reagan's communication skills were not limited to domestic issues. He also used his talent on the international stage. One of the most famous moments of his presidency was when he stood at the Berlin Wall in 1987 and implored the Soviet leader, Mikhail Gorbachev, to "tear down this wall!" This powerful phrase became synonymous with the end of the Cold War.

Reagan's leadership in communication was not solely about eloquence; it was about his ability to convey a clear vision, instill confidence in the American people, and inspire them to work towards a common goal. His speeches and communication style continue to be studied and admired as a masterclass in effective leadership through communication.

Applying Communication

"Communication - the human connection - is the key to personal and career success." - Paul J. Meyer

1. How can you improve clarity and simplicity in communication to ensure that your message is easily understood by the team or audience?

_____

_____

_____

2. In what ways can you use storytelling and memorable anecdotes to make messages more engaging and relatable, as Churchill and Reagan did?

_____

_____

_____

3. How can you effectively use optimism and hope in your communication to inspire and motivate the team, especially during challenging times?

_____

_____

_____

4. What strategies can you employ to adapt your communication style to different audiences and situations, ensuring that your message is relevant and impactful?

_____

_____

_____

5. How can you respond to criticism and opposition with grace and persuasive communication, maintaining support and trust among your team or followers?

_____

_____

_____

6. What role does ethical communication play in your leadership? How can you balance the need for persuasion with honesty and integrity in your messages?

_____

_____

_____

7. In what ways can you use your communication skills to effectively convey a sense of vision and purpose, aligning your team or organization toward common goals?

_____

_____

_____

8. Reflecting on the lessons from Churchill and Reagan, what specific actions can you take to continuously develop and enhance your communication skills as a leader?

_____

_____

_____

Unit 10
The Power of Accountability

"Accountability is the glue that ties commitment to the result."
- Bob Proctor

In leadership, accountability stands as a cornerstone, forging the path towards success and growth. It is the unwavering commitment to taking ownership of our actions, decisions, and their consequences. As leaders, we must recognize that our actions have a profound impact on our team, organization, and the world around us. Embracing accountability is not only about acknowledging our triumphs but also confronting our failures with resilience and a willingness to learn.

In this Unit, we will delve into the essence of accountability in leadership and its transformative power. We will explore how holding ourselves and others accountable fosters a culture of trust, transparency, and collaboration. Through real-life examples and reflective exercises, we will discover how accountability elevates our leadership to new heights and empowers us to lead with integrity and authenticity.

Together, let us embark on this journey of personal and professional growth as we unlock the true potential of accountability in leadership. It is time to embrace the power of accountability and steer our teams towards a future of success, where responsibility and trust reign supreme.

Attributes of Accountability

"Leadership is taking responsibility while others are making excuses." - John C. Maxwell

Honesty and integrity: Leaders with accountability must be honest and truthful in their actions and decisions. They should also hold themselves to the same high standards they expect from others.

Responsibility: Leaders with accountability take responsibility for their actions and decisions, and they hold themselves accountable for any mistakes or failures. They don't blame others or make excuses.

Transparency: Leaders with accountability are transparent in their communication and decision-making processes. They are open to feedback and willing to admit when they don't have all the answers.

Reliability: Leaders with accountability are dependable and can be counted on to follow through on their commitments. They deliver on promises and meet deadlines.

Ownership: Leaders with accountability take ownership of their roles and responsibilities. They are invested in the success of their team and organization and work to make it happen.

Empathy: Leaders with accountability understand the impact of their decisions on others and show empathy towards those affected by their actions. They consider the perspectives and feelings of others in their decision-making.

Adaptability: Leaders with accountability are flexible and adaptable in their approach. They are open to change and willing to adjust their plans when necessary.

Courage: Leaders with accountability have the courage to make tough decisions and take risks when necessary. They are willing to challenge the status quo and make difficult choices for the good of the organization.

Demonstrating Accountability

"Accountability separates the wishers in life from the action-takers that care enough about their future to account for their daily actions." - John Di Lemme

1. What does accountability mean in leadership?

_____

_____

_____

2. How does accountability affect the overall success of a team or organization?

_____

_____

_____

3. What are some traits and characteristics of a leader who takes accountability for their actions and decisions?

_____

_____

_____

4. How does a leader establish a culture of accountability within their team or organization?

_____

_____

_____

5. How does accountability relate to trust and respect in a team or organization?

_____

_____

_____

6. Can accountability be taught and learned, or is it an innate trait?

_____

_____

_____

7. How does a leader balance accountability with giving their team members autonomy and empowerment?

_____

_____

_____

8. How can a leader hold others accountable without being seen as authoritarian or controlling?

_____

_____

_____

9. How can a leader navigate accountability when there are external factors beyond their control that affect the success of the team or organization?

_____

_____

_____

10. What are some common mistakes leaders make when it comes to accountability, and how can they avoid them?

_____

_____

_____

A Leader's Journey from Crisis to Accountability

"Accountability breeds response-ability." - Stephen R. Covey

Anne Mulcahy is a perfect example of a leader who embodies accountability in her actions and decisions. Mulcahy started her career in the Xerox Corporation as a field sales representative in 1976. She gradually rose through the ranks of the company, holding various leadership positions, and became the CEO of Xerox in 2001.

At the time of her appointment, Xerox was in dire financial straits, with a massive debt of and the threat of bankruptcy looming. Mulcahy, along with her team, immediately set to work on a comprehensive restructuring plan to bring the company back to profitability. She made some tough decisions, including laying off thousands of employees and divesting non-core businesses, all while facing criticism and scrutiny from stakeholders.

Despite the challenges and setbacks, Mulcahy stayed committed to her goals and never wavered in her accountability to the company and its stakeholders. She communicated openly and honestly with employees, shareholders, and customers, acknowledging the mistakes of the past and outlining a clear path forward.

Under Mulcahy's leadership, Xerox underwent a remarkable transformation and returned to profitability. She was credited with turning around the company's fortunes and restoring its reputation as an innovator in the printing and document management industry.

Mulcahy's leadership demonstrated the importance of accountability in a leader's decision-making process. By taking ownership of the company's challenges and holding herself and her team responsible for their actions, she was able to lead Xerox through a difficult period and emerge as a successful and respected leader.

Exemplifying Accountability in Leadership

"A true leader has the confidence to stand alone, the courage to make tough decisions, and the compassion to listen to the needs of others." - Douglas MacArthur

Doug Conant's journey to becoming a symbol of accountability in corporate leadership is both inspiring and transformative. His story demonstrates the profound impact that personal accountability can have on an organization's culture and success.

In 2001, Doug Conant assumed the role of CEO at the Campbell Soup Company. At that time, the company was facing a slew of challenges, including declining stock prices, low employee morale, and a struggling corporate culture. Conant recognized that he needed to initiate significant changes to revive Campbell's fortunes.

One of Conant's first moves as CEO was to introduce a unique and highly personal initiative known as "The Campbell Promise." This program was a testament to his unwavering commitment to accountability and his belief in the power of acknowledging the efforts of employees.

"The Campbell Promise" was a simple yet impactful concept. Doug Conant decided to write handwritten thank-you notes to employees who had contributed positively to the company. These notes were not just generic expressions of gratitude; they were heartfelt and specific acknowledgments of individual contributions.

What made this initiative truly remarkable was its scale. Doug Conant personally wrote over 30,000 thank-you notes during his tenure as CEO. This meant that he devoted a significant portion of his time to recognizing and appreciating the efforts of Campbell's workforce. It was a tangible demonstration of his belief that leaders should be accountable for recognizing and valuing their employees.

This commitment to accountability did more than boost employee morale; it transformed the company's culture. Employees felt valued, appreciated, and motivated to contribute their best to the organization. As a result, Campbell Soup Company began to see improvements in performance, innovation, and overall corporate health.

Under Conant's leadership, Campbell's stock price rebounded, and the company's reputation was restored. His approach to accountability was not just a feel-good gesture but a strategic move that translated into tangible results. He understood that when leaders take responsibility for recognizing and appreciating their team, it fosters a culture of accountability and ownership throughout the organization.

Doug Conant's legacy as a leader who understood the profound power of accountability continues to inspire leaders across industries. His story serves as a testament to the idea that recognizing and appreciating the contributions of others is not only a noble act but also a powerful catalyst for positive change within an organization. It reminds us that accountability, when practiced genuinely and consistently, can be a transformational force in leadership.

Applying Accountability

"A good leader takes a little more than his share of the blame, a little less than his share of the credit." - Arnold H. Glas

1. Reflecting on the story of Wilma Anne Mulcahy, who took personal accountability for a challenging situation, how has personal accountability played a role in your own leadership journey?

_____

_____

_____

2. In the case of Doug Conant, he demonstrated accountability by personally writing thousands of thank-you notes to employees. How do you practice accountability in recognizing and appreciating your team's efforts?

_____

_____

_____

3. How do you balance personal and professional accountability in your leadership role??

_____

_____

_____

4. Accountability often involves taking responsibility for both successes and failures. Can you share an instance where you embraced accountability in the face of a challenge, and what were the outcomes?

_____

_____

_____

5. Accountability is not a one-time effort but an ongoing commitment. What strategies do you employ to sustain a culture of accountability within your team or organization over the long term?

_____

_____

_____

Unit 11
The Power of Adaptability

"The measure of intelligence is the ability to change."
- Albert Einstein

In today's fast-paced and ever-changing world, adaptability has become an essential quality for leaders. It is no longer enough for leaders to simply have a sharp vision and set goals. They must also be able to quickly adapt and respond to new challenges, opportunities, and changes in the environment around them.

Leaders who can adapt effectively are able to navigate uncertainty and change with ease, and they are better equipped to lead their teams through challenging times. They are not afraid to experiment, take risks, and learn from their mistakes. They are open-minded, flexible, and able to see the bigger picture.

Adaptability is not just about reacting to change but also about proactively anticipating and preparing for it. Leaders who can identify emerging trends and technologies and pivot their strategies accordingly can position their organizations for long-term success.

But adaptability is not always easy. It requires a willingness to challenge assumptions, let go of old habits, and embrace current ideas. It also requires a certain level of resilience, as leaders may face setbacks and failures along the way.

In this Unit, we will explore the importance of adaptability in leadership and look at examples of leaders who have shown this quality effectively. We will also delve into the characteristics and traits of leaders who are adaptable and provide practical tips for developing this essential skillset.

Attributes of Adaptability

"Adaptability is being able to adjust to any situation at any given time." - John Wooden

Flexibility: Adaptable leaders are flexible and open-minded, willing to consider different perspectives and approaches to problem-solving.

Resilience: These leaders have a keen sense of resilience, able to bounce back from setbacks and failures quickly and effectively.

Creativity: Adaptable leaders are creative and innovative, able to think outside the box and find innovative solutions to old problems.

Emotional intelligence: These leaders have elevated levels of emotional intelligence and are able to recognize and manage their own emotions as well as those of others.

Continuous learning: Adaptable leaders are committed to continuous learning and self-improvement, always seeking out new knowledge and skills to stay ahead of the curve.

Risk-taking: These leaders are comfortable taking risks and making bold decisions, even in the face of uncertainty.

Agility: Adaptable leaders are agile and able to shift priorities, plans, and strategies quickly and easily in response to changing circumstances.

Visionary: These leaders have a clear and compelling vision for the future but are also able to adjust and adapt that vision as needed to meet new challenges and opportunities.

Demonstrating Adaptability

"Adaptability is being able to adjust to any situation at any given time, while maintaining a positive attitude and flexible nature."
- Unknown

1. How can leaders foster a culture of adaptability within their organizations?

_____

_____

_____

2. What are some common barriers to adaptability, and how can leaders overcome them?

_____

_____

_____

3. How do adaptable leaders balance the need for stability and consistency with the need for flexibility and agility?

_____

_____

_____

4. In what ways do adaptable leaders respond to changing circumstances and unexpected challenges?

_____

_____

_____

5. How can leaders assess their own level of adaptability and identify areas for improvement?

_____

_____

_____

6. How can leaders balance the competing demands of adapting to change and keeping a clear sense of direction and vision for their organization?

_____

_____

_____

7. How do adaptable leaders remain resilient and persistent in the face of setbacks and challenges?

_____

_____

_____

The Power of Adaptability in Leadership

"Leadership is not about staying the same; it's about evolving and leading others through change." - Unknown

Phil Jackson, the former head coach of the Chicago Bulls and the Los Angeles Lakers in the NBA, was known for his ability to adapt his coaching style to fit the strengths and weaknesses of his players. He led the Bulls and the Lakers to multiple championships by implementing a unique basketball style emphasizing teamwork and collaboration.

One example of Jackson's adaptability came during the 1995-1996 season with the Bulls. The team had lost its star player, Michael Jordan, to retirement and was struggling to find its footing. Jackson adapted by changing the team's offensive strategy, focusing more on ball movement and player involvement rather than relying solely on Jordan's individual brilliance. This new strategy led the Bulls to a record-breaking 72-win season and an NBA championship.

Another example came during the 2008-2009 season with the Lakers. Jackson recognized that his star player, Kobe Bryant, was dominating the ball too much and not involving his teammates enough. Jackson adapted by implementing a new offense that emphasized more ball movement and player involvement, which led to the Lakers winning the NBA championship that season.

Jackson's ability to adapt his coaching style to fit the strengths and weaknesses of his players allowed him to achieve remarkable success in his career and cemented his legacy as one of the greatest coaches in NBA history.

Adaptability in Extreme Conditions

"Adaptability is about the powerful difference between adapting to cope and adapting to win." - Max McKeown

Ernest Shackleton led an expedition to cross Antarctica in 1914. The journey was beset with challenges, including the ship getting stuck in ice and eventually sinking, leaving the crew stranded in harsh conditions.

Despite the dire situation, Shackleton showed remarkable adaptability in his leadership. He quickly realized that the mission of crossing Antarctica was no longer possible and instead focused on the goal of getting his entire crew back to civilization alive.

To achieve this goal, Shackleton and his crew had to adapt to the extreme conditions of the Antarctic. They camped on floating ice for months, made perilous journeys on foot and in small boats, and endured harsh weather conditions. Shackleton also had to adapt his leadership style to motivate and encourage his crew in the face of such adversity.

Through his adaptability, Shackleton was able to lead his crew through one of the most remarkable survival stories in history. All members of the expedition eventually returned home safely, with no loss of life. Shackleton's leadership serves as a powerful example of the importance of adaptability in leadership, especially in challenging situations.

Applying Adaptability

"Adaptability is the key to effective leadership. Embrace change with open arms and a willing heart." - Unknown

1. How does the adaptability demonstrated in these stories resonate with your own experiences as a leader?

_____

_____

_____

2. Reflect on a challenging situation in your leadership journey where adaptability played a crucial role. What was the outcome, and what did you learn from it?

_____

_____

_____

3. In what ways have you had to pivot or adjust your strategies when faced with unexpected obstacles or changes in your leadership role?

_____

_____

_____

4. Think about a time when you needed to lead a team through uncertainty. How did you apply adaptability to navigate the ambiguity and keep your team on course?

_____

_____

_____

5. Consider the importance of adaptability when working with diverse teams or individuals with varying strengths and backgrounds. How do you tailor your leadership style to accommodate these differences?

_____

_____

_____

6. Reflect on a leadership challenge where you had to learn from past failures and adapt your approach. What specific adjustments did you make, and what were the results?

_____

_____

_____

7. Think about how mindfulness or being present in the moment has influenced your ability to adapt to changing circumstances as a leader. Can you share an instance where this was particularly valuable?

_____

_____

_____

8. In your leadership journey, how has adaptability become an integral part of your leadership style and a core competency? How do you encourage its development in your team or organization?

_____

_____

_____

Unit 12
The Power of Collaboration

"Alone, we can do so little; together, we can do so much."
- Helen Keller

In the ever-evolving landscape of leadership, one trait stands as a beacon of progress and success: collaboration. As leaders, we are tasked with guiding our teams towards greatness, and collaboration serves as the driving force that propels us forward. It is the art of harnessing the collective wisdom, skills, and diverse perspectives of our team members to create a unified force with boundless potential.

In this Unit, we will embark on a journey to explore the profound impact of collaboration in leadership. We will uncover the transformative power that arises when leaders foster an environment of open communication, trust, and inclusivity. Through real-life stories of leaders who embraced collaboration, we will witness how their teams achieved remarkable feats, overcoming challenges that once seemed insurmountable.

We will dive into the strategies and practices that empower leaders to inspire their teams to collaborate effectively, breaking down barriers and nurturing a culture of synergy. This Unit will be a treasure trove of insights, reflective exercises, and practical tools that will help you unlock the full potential of collaboration in your leadership journey.

Join me as we unravel the secret to becoming a collaborative leader, igniting the spark of innovation, and fostering a sense of unity that leads us to unparalleled success. Together, we will explore the dynamic interplay between leadership and collaboration, uncovering the path towards a future where great leaders and great teams stand side by side, driven by a shared vision and a passion for excellence.

Attributes of Collaboration

"Coming together is a beginning; keeping together is progress; working together is success." - Henry Ford

Open-mindedness: Collaborative leaders are open to different ideas, perspectives, and feedback from team members. They value diversity of thought and actively seek input from others.

Effective communication: Collaborative leaders possess strong communication skills, actively listening to others, expressing ideas clearly, and fostering open and honest dialogue. They ensure that everyone understands the goals, expectations, and roles within the collaboration.

Relationship-building: Collaborative leaders invest time and effort in building strong relationships with team members. They foster a sense of trust, respect, and mutual support, creating a safe and inclusive environment for collaboration.

Empathy: Collaborative leaders demonstrate empathy by understanding and considering the needs, feelings, and perspectives of others. They create an atmosphere where everyone feels valued and heard, promoting a sense of psychological safety within the team.

Conflict resolution:-Collaborative leaders are skilled in managing conflicts that may arise within a collaborative setting. They approach conflicts with a constructive mindset, seeking win-win solutions and encouraging open dialogue to reach consensus.

Delegation: Collaborative leaders understand the importance of delegating tasks and responsibilities to team members. They empower others by providing them with autonomy and trusting them to contribute their skills and ability to the collaboration.

Shared accountability: A collaborative leader fosters a sense of shared accountability among team members. They encourage everyone to take ownership of their roles and responsibilities, ensuring that the entire team is committed to achieving shared goals.

Flexibility: A collaborative leader is adaptable and flexible in their approach. They understand that collaboration requires adjusting plans, embracing current ideas, and being open to change as the team progresses toward its goals.

Appreciation and recognition: Collaborative leaders value and acknowledge the contributions of team members. They celebrate achievements, express gratitude, and recognize the efforts of individuals, fostering a positive and motivating environment.

Long-term focus: Collaborative leaders look beyond short-term wins and aim for long-term success. They prioritize building sustainable relationships, fostering a collaborative culture, and creating opportunities for ongoing collaboration and growth.

Demonstrating Collaboration

"Collaboration is the key that unlocks the door to exceptional results." - Unknown

1. How does open-mindedness contribute to effective collaboration as a leader?

_____

_____

_____

2. In what ways can effective communication enhance collaboration within a team?

_____

_____

_____

3. How can a leader build strong relationships with team members to foster collaboration?

_____

_____

_____

4. Why is empathy important in promoting collaboration and creating a positive team environment?

_____

_____

_____

5. How can a leader effectively manage conflicts that arise during the collaboration process?

_____

_____

_____

6. Why is delegation an essential trait for a leader to foster collaboration within a team?

_____

_____

_____

7. How does shared accountability contribute to successful collaboration within a team?

_____

_____

_____

8. In what ways can a leader demonstrate flexibility in his or her approach to enhance collaboration?

_____

_____

_____

9. How can a leader show appreciation and recognize team members to encourage collaboration?

_____

_____

_____

10. Why is having a long-term focus important for a leader in fostering a collaborative culture?

_____

_____

_____

Bridging Divides: A Story of Collaborative Leadership

"Collaboration is the foundation of great leadership." - Unknown

Abraham Lincoln, the 16th President of the United States, is widely regarded as one of the greatest leaders in American history. During his presidency, he faced the daunting challenge of leading a nation torn apart by the Civil War. However, Lincoln's collaborative leadership style played a pivotal role in uniting the country and ultimately leading to the abolition of slavery.

One notable example of Lincoln's collaborative leadership was his approach to forming his Cabinet. Rather than surrounding himself with loyalists or individuals who shared the same viewpoints as he had, Lincoln intentionally assembled a diverse group of individuals from different political parties and backgrounds. He recognized that to effectively lead the nation through such a crisis, he needed the input and expertise of those with differing perspectives.

Lincoln fostered a culture of open dialogue and encouraged his Cabinet members to freely express their opinions and engage in vigorous debates. He valued their expertise and believed that by embracing differing viewpoints, he could make more informed decisions. Lincoln was known to listen attentively to the arguments of his advisors, asking probing questions and seeking consensus whenever possible.

One of the most significant instances of Lincoln's collaborative leadership was the Emancipation Proclamation. While Lincoln had long been personally committed to ending slavery, he understood the importance of building consensus and garnering support for such a monumental decision. He engaged in extensive discussions with his Cabinet and sought their counsel before issuing the proclamation. Through collaboration and careful consideration, Lincoln was able to rally support and pave the way for the eventual passage of the 13th Amendment, which formally abolished slavery in the United States.

Lincoln's collaborative approach extended beyond his Cabinet. He also engaged with military leaders, members of Congress, and even his political opponents in an effort to bring about national unity. He understood that the challenges facing the nation required collective effort and collaboration from all sectors of society.

Lincoln's collaborative leadership played a crucial role in guiding the nation through the Civil War and bringing about significant societal change. His ability to harness the collective wisdom and diverse perspectives of those around him exemplifies the power of collaboration in leadership. Lincoln's collaborative approach not only helped him navigate a divided nation but also laid the foundation for a more inclusive and equal society.

Strategies for Success: A Collaborative Approach

"When you collaborate, you elevate everyone's potential."
- Unknown

Warren Buffett, often referred to as the "Oracle of Omaha," is not only known for his remarkable investment prowess but also for his collaborative leadership style. His partnership with Charlie Munger, Vice Chairman of Berkshire Hathaway, exemplifies his commitment to collaboration.

One aspect of Buffett's collaborative leadership is his recognition of his own limitations. While he is a legendary investor, he acknowledges that he doesn't possess expertise in every industry or area of business. Instead of trying to go it alone, he seeks out experts in those fields.

For instance, when Berkshire Hathaway acquired See's Candies in 1972, Buffett brought in Charles Huggins, a skilled manager with a background in the confectionery industry, to run the company. He recognized that while he could assess the financial aspects of the business, he needed someone with specialized knowledge to lead it effectively.

Buffett's approach to investing also embodies collaboration. He often engages with company management when Berkshire Hathaway takes a substantial stake in a company. Rather than imposing his will, he works alongside them and provides support when necessary. His reputation for long-term, patient capital is appealing to many business leaders who appreciate his collaborative approach to stewarding their companies.

Another key element of Buffett's collaborative leadership is his partnership with Charlie Munger. The two have worked together for decades, with Munger serving as Buffett's sounding board and vice versa. They have complementary skills— Buffett is known for his value investing acumen, while Munger has a broad knowledge of various disciplines. Their annual shareholder meetings, known as the "Woodstock for Capitalists," are famous for their candid discussions and insights.

Buffett's collaborative style extends to his mentoring relationships. He has mentored and influenced numerous business leaders and investors over the years, sharing his wisdom and experience generously.

Warren Buffett's collaborative leadership style is characterized by recognizing his own limitations, seeking out experts, working alongside company management, and fostering long-term partnerships with individuals like Charlie Munger. Through collaboration, he has built Berkshire Hathaway into a conglomerate of successful businesses and created lasting value for shareholders.

Applying Collaboration

"If everyone is moving forward together, then success takes care of itself." -
Henry Ford

1. Can you share an instance from your leadership experience where collaboration played a significant role in achieving a challenging goal? What did this experience teach you about the power of working together?

_____

_____

_____

2. Think about the importance of building trust among team members to enable effective collaboration. Can you describe an example of when trust-building efforts paid off in your leadership journey?

_____

_____

_____

3. Collaboration often involves active listening and empathy. Share a story of how your ability to listen and understand the needs of your team members contributed to a collaborative success.

_____

_____

_____

4. Think about the role of effective communication in collaboration. Can you recall an experience where clear communication was pivotal in bringing about a collaborative achievement?

_____

_____

_____

5. Both leaders in these stories had the ability to inspire and motivate others toward a shared vision. How do you inspire a sense of purpose and collaboration among your team members?

_____

_____

_____

Unit 13
The Power of Inclusion

"Inclusion is not a matter of political correctness. It is the key to unlocking the full potential of our people and organizations."
- Melinda Gates

Inclusion is not just a buzzword; it is a fundamental value that can transform individuals, organizations, and societies. It goes beyond mere diversity and takes a step further towards creating an environment where every individual feels valued, respected, and empowered. The power of inclusion lies in recognizing and embracing the unique perspectives, experiences, and contributions of every person, regardless of their background or identity. It is about fostering a sense of belonging, where everyone has an equal opportunity to participate, contribute, and succeed.

In this Unit, we will explore the concept of inclusion and its profound impact on leadership. We will delve into the importance of creating an inclusive culture, the benefits it brings to individuals and organizations, and the strategies leaders can employ to promote inclusion. Through inspiring stories and practical insights, we will discover how leaders can cultivate an inclusive mindset, build diverse teams, and create an environment where everyone thrives. Join us on this journey as we explore the transformative power of inclusion in leadership.

Attributes of Inclusion

"Inclusion is not a trend, it's a mindset. It's about creating a culture where everyone feels heard, valued, and empowered."
- Unknown

Open-mindedness: Inclusive leaders possess open minds and are receptive to different perspectives and ideas. They actively seek out diverse opinions and viewpoints to make informed decisions and create an inclusive environment.

Empathy: Leaders who prioritize inclusion demonstrate empathy towards others. They genuinely understand and care about the experiences, feelings, and needs of their team members. This empathy allows them to connect on a deeper level and create a sense of belonging.

Active Listening: Inclusive leaders are skilled listeners. They actively engage in listening to understand rather than just responding. They create a safe space for others to express themselves and ensure that everyone's voice is heard and valued.

Collaboration: Leaders who promote inclusion understand the power of collaboration. They foster a collaborative culture where individuals work together, leveraging their diverse skills and experiences to achieve shared goals.

Equity and Fairness: Inclusive leaders prioritize fairness and equity. They ensure that everyone has equal opportunities for growth and development, regardless of their background or identity. They actively address biases and work to remove systemic barriers that hinder inclusion.

Cultural Competence: Leaders who embrace inclusion are culturally competent. They appreciate and respect diverse cultural norms, values, and practices. They strive to create an environment where diversity is celebrated and individuals can bring their whole selves to work.

Transparent Communication: Inclusive leaders practice transparent communication. They keep their team members well-informed about important decisions, changes, and opportunities. They communicate openly and honestly, building trust and fostering a sense of inclusion.

Growth Mindset: Leaders who prioritize inclusion have a growth mindset. They recognize that inclusion is an ongoing journey and are committed to continuous learning and improvement. They are open to feedback and are willing to adapt their approaches to create a more inclusive environment.

Courageous Advocacy: Inclusive leaders are courageous advocates for inclusion. They actively challenge biases, stereotypes, and discriminatory practices. They stand up for the rights and dignity of all individuals, creating a safe and inclusive space for everyone.

Resilience: Leaders who champion inclusion demonstrate resilience. They navigate challenges and setbacks with determination and perseverance. They do not give up in the face of resistance or adversity and continue to champion inclusion as a core value.

Demonstrating Inclusion

"True leaders understand the power of inclusion. They know that when everyone's voices are heard, the collective wisdom and creativity can propel their organization forward." - Unknown

1. What does it mean to have an open-minded approach as a leader, and how does it contribute to fostering inclusion?

_____

_____

_____

2. How can empathy play a role in building an inclusive environment, and why is it important for leaders to demonstrate empathy toward their team members?

_____

_____

_____

3. In what ways can active listening enhance the inclusivity of a team, and how can leaders practice active listening effectively?

_____

_____

_____

4. How does collaboration contribute to creating an inclusive culture within a team or organization, and what are some strategies leaders can use to encourage collaboration?

_____

_____

_____

5. Why are equity and fairness crucial for fostering inclusion, and how can leaders ensure equal opportunities for growth and development?

_____

_____

_____

6. What does it mean to be culturally competent as a leader, and how can cultural competence enhance inclusion within a diverse team?

_____

_____

_____

7. How does transparent communication contribute to an inclusive environment, and what are some effective communication practices leaders can adopt?

_____

_____

_____

8. How does having a growth mindset support leaders in promoting and advancing inclusion within their teams or organizations?

_____

_____

_____

9. Why is courageous advocacy important for leaders in fostering inclusion, and how can leaders effectively advocate for inclusion?

_____

_____

_____

10. How does resilience play a role in promoting and sustaining an inclusive culture, and what are some strategies leaders can use to foster resilience within their teams?

_____

_____

_____

Breaking Barriers: A Journey of Inclusion and Leadership

"The strongest teams are built on the foundation of inclusion. When everyone feels valued and included, they bring their best selves to work, and together, they can achieve extraordinary results." - Unknown

Ellen Kullman, the former CEO of DuPont, is an exemplary leader who championed the importance of inclusion in the workplace. Throughout her tenure, she recognized the need for diversity and gender equality within the company and took proactive steps to drive change.

Under Kullman's leadership, DuPont implemented various initiatives to promote inclusivity and create a more diverse workforce. One notable program she introduced was the Women's Network, which aimed to support and develop women leaders within the organization. The network provided mentorship, networking opportunities, and professional development resources to help women advance in their careers.

Kullman also recognized the significance of diverse perspectives in driving innovation and problem-solving. She encouraged open dialogue and collaboration among employees, fostering an environment where everyone felt comfortable expressing their ideas and opinions. This inclusive culture not only enhanced employee engagement and job satisfaction but also contributed to the company's success in developing innovative solutions for its customers. Dupont ensures that its product offerings cater to a wide range of industries and customers, considering the diverse needs and requirements of different markets. By actively involving customers from various backgrounds in the development process, Dupont creates inclusive solutions that address specific challenges faced by different communities.

In addition to internal initiatives, Kullman actively engaged with external organizations and communities to promote inclusion and diversity. She served on the board of Catalyst, a nonprofit organization advocating for women's advancement in the workplace. Through her involvement, Kullman had a broader impact on advancing the cause of inclusivity beyond the boundaries of DuPont.

Kullman's commitment to inclusion extended beyond gender equality. She recognized the importance of embracing diversity in all its forms, including race, ethnicity, age, and background. By valuing and leveraging the unique perspectives and experiences of individuals from diverse backgrounds, she believed that DuPont could better serve its customers, drive innovation, and create a more inclusive society.

Through her leadership, Ellen Kullman demonstrated that fostering an inclusive culture is not just the right thing to do ethically, but it is also a strategic imperative for the success of the organization. Her commitment to diversity and inclusion left a lasting impact on DuPont and serves as an inspiration for leaders seeking to create inclusive workplaces where every individual is empowered to thrive.

A Trailblazing Journey Toward Inclusive Leadership

"Inclusion is a leadership mindset that recognizes and appreciates the diverse strengths and perspectives of individuals, creating a culture where everyone can thrive." - Unknown

Melinda Gates, co-founder of the Bill & Melinda Gates Foundation, has been a prominent leader in advocating for inclusion and equal access to opportunities. Through her philanthropic work, she has focused on addressing global health issues, poverty alleviation, and improving education systems worldwide.

One of the key initiatives led by Melinda Gates is the Gender Equality program of the Bill & Melinda Gates Foundation. She has been a vocal advocate for gender equality, recognizing the importance of empowering women and girls and ensuring their inclusion in all aspects of society. She has championed efforts to advance women's rights, eliminate gender-based discrimination, and provide women with equal opportunities to succeed.

In addition to her work in promoting gender equality, Melinda has also emphasized the importance of inclusivity in global health and development. She has been committed to ensuring that the most marginalized and vulnerable populations have access to healthcare, education, and economic opportunities. She recognizes that true progress can only be achieved by including and uplifting those who are often left behind.

Melinda has used her leadership platform to amplify the voices of marginalized communities and advocate for policies and investments that promote inclusivity. She has worked closely with governments, NGOs, and grassroots organizations to drive positive change and create a more inclusive world.

Through her leadership, Melinda has demonstrated a deep understanding of the power of inclusion and its transformative impact on individuals and communities. Her dedication to inclusivity serves as an inspiration to leaders around the world, encouraging them to prioritize diversity, equity, and inclusion in their own spheres of influence.

Applying Inclusion

"Diversity is being invited to the party; inclusion is being asked to dance." -
Verna Myers

1. Inclusion often requires actively seeking out diverse perspectives. How do you ensure that different voices are heard and valued within your team or organization, similar to the leaders in these stories??

_____

_____

_____

2. Both stories highlight the importance of diversity and inclusion in achieving success. Can you share an example from your experience where embracing diversity and fostering inclusion led to positive outcomes within your team or organization??

_____

_____

_____

3. Inclusion often requires actively seeking out diverse perspectives. How do you ensure that different voices are heard and valued within your team or organization, similar to the leaders in these stories?

_____

_____

_____

4. Inclusion often requires addressing biases and stereotypes. How do you work to challenge and mitigate unconscious biases within your team or organization?

_____

_____

_____

5. What are some potential challenges you may face in promoting inclusion, and how can you address them?

_____

_____

_____

6. How can you continuously educate yourself and stay informed about current issues and best practices related to inclusion in leadership?

_____

_____

_____

10. How will you measure the success of your efforts to promote inclusion and ensure that it remains a priority on your leadership journey?

_____

_____

_____

Unit 14
The Power of Mentorship

"The delicate balance of mentoring someone is not creating them in your own image but giving them the opportunity to create themselves." - Steven Spielberg

Throughout our lives, we encounter challenges and obstacles that can make the journey to success feel daunting. But having a mentor by our side can make all the difference.

A mentor is someone who possesses a wealth of experience and knowledge and is considered a trusted advisor in their field. A mentor is someone who guides, supports, and offers valuable insights and advice to a less experienced individual (the mentee) in their personal or professional development. Mentors are often sought out by individuals who are looking to enhance their skills, advance their careers, or achieve their personal goals.

Mentors usually have extensive experience in a particular area or field, and they are willing to share their knowledge, skills, and expertise to help their mentees achieve their full potential. They provide guidance and support in various areas, such as developing new skills, navigating professional challenges, and managing career transitions.

Mentoring is a two-way relationship, with the mentor and mentee working together to achieve specific goals. Mentors may offer coaching, feedback, and networking opportunities to their mentees. They may also provide guidance on career development, leadership, and personal growth.

Effective mentoring requires a positive and supportive relationship between the mentor and the mentee. Mentors must create a safe and open environment where the mentee feels comfortable discussing their challenges and seeking advice.

Mentors must also set clear goals and expectations and provide ongoing feedback and encouragement to keep the mentee motivated.

In this Unit, we'll explore the power of mentorship and how it can transform your personal and professional life. We will look at the benefits of having a mentor, how to find the right mentor, and how to build a strong and meaningful relationship with him or her. Whether you're just starting out in your career or looking to take it to the next level, this Unit will provide you with the tools and insights you need to succeed with the help of a mentor.

Attributes of a Mentor

"A mentor is someone who believes in you, encourages you, and helps you become the best version of yourself." - Unknown

Provides guidance and support: A mentor provides guidance and support to the mentee, drawing on their own experiences and knowledge to help the mentee achieve their goals.

Offers feedback and advice: A mentor provides constructive feedback and advice to the mentee, helping them to name areas for improvement and make progress towards their goals.

Acts as a sounding board: A mentor listens to the mentee's ideas and concerns and provides a safe space for them to discuss their thoughts and feelings.

Shares experiences and expertise: A mentor shares their own experiences and expertise with the mentee, providing insights and perspectives that the mentee may not have considered.

Encourages personal and professional growth: A mentor encourages the mentee to challenge themselves, take risks, and pursue opportunities for personal and professional growth.

Provides networking opportunities: A mentor introduces the mentee to other professionals in their network, helping them to build their own professional connections and expand their opportunities.

Helps develop new skills: A mentor helps the mentee develop new skills and knowledge, providing training, resources, and support as needed.

Supports career development: A mentor helps the mentee to identify their career goals and develop a plan to achieve them.

Provides motivation and inspiration: A mentor provides motivation and inspiration to the mentee, helping them to stay focused and motivated on their goals.

Respects confidentiality: A mentor respects the mentee's privacy and confidentiality, ensuring that any sensitive information shared during the mentoring relationship is kept confidential.

Demonstrating Mentorship

"To mentor someone is to affirm their worth and potential."
- Unknown

1. What are some key qualities or attributes that make a successful mentor?

_____
_____
_____

2. How can a mentor create a supportive and trusting relationship with their mentee?

_____
_____
_____

3. What are some effective strategies for a mentor to provide guidance and feedback to their mentee?

_____
_____
_____

4. How can a mentor help their mentee identify and work towards their goals?

_____
_____
_____

5. What are some ways a mentor can help their mentee develop new skills or enhance existing ones?

_____

_____

_____

6. How can a mentor encourage their mentee to step out of their comfort zone and take on new challenges?

_____

_____

_____

My First Mentor

"The art of mentoring is not about creating a replica of oneself but providing opportunities for individuals to create their own unique path." - Steven Spielberg

My mother was an extraordinary woman who triumphed over multiple obstacles while holding steadfast to her beliefs. Her teachings have had a lasting influence on me, emphasizing the importance of family, integrity, and always staying true to myself. She stressed the significance of continuous learning and resilience when confronting challenges, instilling in me a desire to seek out opportunities for personal growth and development.

During her battle with ovarian cancer, I was in awe of my mother's unbreakable courage and determination. Despite the challenges she faced, she refused to allow her illness to define her. Each day, she would wake up early, don her wig and makeup, and dress impeccably to take on the day. Whenever people asked her if she ever wondered why she was the one battling ovarian cancer, my mother's response was always, "Why not me?" She passionately believed that once you understood the challenge you were facing, you could approach it with confidence and energy.

My mother's selflessness and love for her family were also evident in her actions. She was always available for us and made us feel loved and valued. Her legacy continues to inspire me, and I will always be grateful for the lessons she taught me.

Unlocking Potential: A Story Guidance

One of the greatest values of mentors is the ability to see ahead what others cannot see and to help them navigate a course to their destination." - John C. Maxwell

Anne Sullivan was a teacher and mentor to Helen Keller, a deaf and blind woman who became a prominent author and activist despite the numerous challenges she faced throughout her life. Sullivan taught Keller how to communicate, provided her with the tools she needed to succeed in life, and played a crucial role in helping Keller overcome these challenges and achieve success.

When Sullivan first met Keller, she was a wild and untamed child who had never learned to communicate with the outside world. Sullivan recognized Keller's potential and was determined to help her develop her abilities.

Sullivan began by teaching Keller how to sign, using her hands to spell out words on Keller's palms. This allowed Keller to communicate with others for the first time in her life, and she quickly became eager to learn as much as she could.

Over the years, Sullivan continued to work with Keller, teaching her how to read, write, and speak. She also helped Keller to develop her talents as a writer and public speaker, encouraging her to share her experiences with others and become an advocate for the deaf and blind community.

Despite facing numerous obstacles and setbacks, Keller remained committed to her education and her goals. With Sullivan's guidance and support, she graduated from Radcliffe College with honors and became a prominent author and activist, traveling the world and speaking out on behalf of people with disabilities.

Throughout their lives, Keller and Sullivan remained close friends and collaborators, with Sullivan serving as a mentor and guide to Keller until her death in 1936. Today, their legacy lives on as a testament to the power of mentorship and the importance of perseverance in the face of adversity.

Applying Mentorship

"Mentorship is the art of unlocking someone's potential and helping them realize their worth." - Unknown

1. What qualities or characteristics do you believe make an effective mentor, based on your own experiences with mentors?

_____

_____

_____

2. Reflecting on your leadership journey, can you share a specific moment or experience where mentorship played a pivotal role in your growth and development as a leader?

_____

_____

_____

3. Can you provide an example of a valuable piece of advice or insight you received from a mentor that had a lasting impact on your leadership approach?

_____

_____

_____

4. How can you embrace mentorship as a lifelong learning process, even when faced with adversities or limitations?

_____

_____

_____

5. What are some practical steps we can take to find mentors and establish meaningful mentorship relationships?

_____

_____

_____

6. How can we become mentors ourselves, offering guidance, support, and empowerment to others on their own journeys?

_____

_____

_____

Maximizing Your Mentorship Experience

"One of the greatest values of mentors is the ability to see ahead what others cannot see and to help them navigate a course to their destination." - John C. Maxwell

Set goals: Before meeting with their mentor, a mentee should set clear goals and objectives for what he or she hopes to achieve from the mentoring relationship. This will help to focus the conversation and ensure that the mentee gets the most out of the time with the mentor.

Review previous discussions: If the mentee has already had meetings with the mentor, they should review their notes and any action items from previous discussions. This will help track progress and ensure the mentee is making progress towards his or her goals.

Prepare questions: The mentee should prepare a list of questions to ask their mentor before the meeting. These questions should be focused on the mentee's goals and objectives and should help to guide the conversation towards actionable steps that the mentee can take to achieve their goals.

Bring materials: If the mentee has any relevant materials, such as a resume, project plans, or performance evaluations, bring these to the meeting. These materials can help to provide context for the conversation and help the mentor provide more specific guidance and advice.

Be open and receptive: The mentee should approach the meeting with an open and receptive attitude. He or she should be willing to listen to their mentor's advice and feedback and should be open to new ideas and perspectives. By approaching the meeting with a positive mindset, the mentee can get the most out of the time with the mentor and make meaningful progress towards goals.

Conclusion

Our exploration through the units on leadership superpowers has been a profound exploration of the qualities and characteristics that define exceptional leaders. These superpowers are not mere concepts but dynamic forces that shape the course of leadership journeys. Let's take a moment to reflect on each of these remarkable superpowers:

Trust is the foundation upon which all leadership is built. It's the glue that binds leaders and their teams, fostering an environment of reliability and confidence.

Respect emerged as the cornerstone of diversity and inclusion. It's the superpower that honors every individual's unique perspective and cultivates a culture of unity.

Integrity is the moral compass that guides leaders through challenging decisions. It's the unwavering commitment to doing what is right, even in the face of adversity.

Empathy emerged as the bridge that connects leaders with their teams on a profound level. It's the ability to understand and relate to others' feelings, creating strong bonds of trust.

Humility was revealed as the strength that allows leaders to admit their vulnerabilities and value the contributions of others. It's the essence of authentic leadership.

Courage emerged as the force that propels leaders to confront challenges head-on. It's the superpower that enables them to take risks, stand for their convictions, and inspire others to do the same.

Resilience is the wellspring of perseverance and determination. It's the ability to bounce back from setbacks, emerging stronger and more capable with each trial.

Empowerment is the catalyst for unleashing the full potential of teams. It's the superpower that enables leaders to nurture the growth and development of those they lead.

Communication is the bridge that connects leaders with their teams, enabling them to convey their vision and foster understanding.

Accountability emerged as the cornerstone of responsibility and transparency. It's the superpower that ensures leaders and their teams are answerable for their actions and decisions.

Adaptability is the ability to thrive in an ever-changing world. It's the superpower that equips leaders with the flexibility to adjust to new circumstances and seize opportunities.

Collaboration is the art of working together synergistically. It's the superpower that transforms diverse talents into collective achievements.

Inclusion is the commitment to creating spaces where every voice is heard. It's the superpower that celebrates diversity and ensures that all individuals are valued and included.

Mentorship is the legacy of knowledge passed down through generations of leaders. It's the superpower that enables experienced leaders to guide and inspire the next wave of visionaries.

Incorporating these superpowers into your leadership journey will empower you to navigate the complexities of the ever-evolving world of leadership. They are not just ideals but actionable principles that can guide your decision-making, your interactions with others, and your impact on the world.

As you move forward in your leadership endeavors, remember that these superpowers are not static; they evolve and strengthen with practice and experience. Embrace them, cultivate them, and share them with those you lead. By doing so, you'll not only become a better leader but also inspire greatness in others.

So, with these leadership superpowers as your guiding lights, go forth and lead with confidence, empathy, and a commitment to positive change. Your journey as a remarkable leader is just beginning, and the world awaits the positive impact you will create.

About the Author

After a successful career in the banking industry spanning more than three decades, Bonnie decided to embark on a new phase as a leadership coach and trainer. She finds this to be one of the most rewarding experiences of her life.

Bonnie was a trailblazer for women in her community, being the first female member and, later, the first female president of the Kiwanis Club of Tampa. She has also been actively involved in various Chambers of Commerce and has dedicated her time to numerous volunteer organizations.

Bonnie is passionate about empowering individuals to reach their full potential by helping them step outside their comfort zones and find direction in their personal and professional lives. In this book, she hopes to share her knowledge and experience in assisting leaders in unlocking their true potential and discovering their unique superpowers.

www.ingramcontent.com/pod-product-compliance
Lightning Source LLC
Chambersburg PA
CBHW041140120626
46547CB00020B/3056